My First Question and Answer Book

My First Question and Answer Book

Miles Kelly

First published in 2007 by Miles Kelly Publishing Ltd
Harding's Barn, Bardfield End Green, Thaxted, Essex, CM6 3PX, UK

Copyright © Miles Kelly Publishing Ltd 2007

This edition printed in 2014

12 14 16 18 19 17 15 13

Publishing Director Belinda Gallagher
Creative Director Jo Cowan
Editorial Assistant Carly Blake
Authors Camilla de la Bedoyere,
Catherine Chambers, Chris Oxlade
Cover Designer Jo Cowan
Designers Jo Brewer, Venita Kidwai,
Sophie Pelham, Elaine Wilkinson, Candice Bekir
Indexer Helen Snaith
Production Manager Elizabeth Collins
Archive Manager Jennifer Hunt
Reprographics Anthony Cambray, Liberty Newton, Ian Paulyn
Assets Lorraine King

The publisher would like to thank iStockphoto.com for the use of the image on page 147

ISBN 978-1-84236-914-2

Printed in China

British Library Cataloguing-in-Publication Data
A catalogue record for this book is available from the British Library

Made with paper from a sustainable forest

www.mileskelly.net
info@mileskelly.net

Contents

Space 8

Planet Earth 38

Oceans 68

Weather 98

Science 128

Inventions 158

Your Body 188

Dinosaurs 218

Bugs 248

Reptiles &
Amphibians 278

Birds 308

Mammals 326

Ancient Egypt 348

Ancient Rome 370

Vikings 400

Knights & Castles 430

Pirates 448

Explorers 470

Index 500

Questions about...

Which star keeps us warm? 10
When is it night time during
   the day? 11
Why is the Sun spotty? 11

Is Earth the only planet near
   the Sun? 12
Do other planets have moons? 13
What are other planets like? 13

What is inside the Earth? 14
Why does the Moon change
   shape? 15
Why do we have day and night? 15

What is the hottest planet? 16
Why is Mars called the
   red planet? 17
Which planet has the biggest
   volcano? 17

Does Pluto have its own moon? 18
Why does Mercury look like
the Moon? 19
Which planet is baking hot and
   freezing cold? 19

What is the biggest planet? 20
Which planet has rings? 21
Is there a giant made of gas? 21

Which planet rolls
   around? 22
Why does
   Neptune look
   so blue? 23
Why do Neptune
and Pluto
swap places? 23

Space

Are there snowballs in space?   24
What is a shooting star?   24
Does the Sun have a belt?   25

How are stars made?   26
What is a group of stars
    called?   27
Are all stars white?   27

What is the Milky Way?   28
Can galaxies crash?   28
Do galaxies have arms?   29

How does a shuttle get
    into space?   30
How fast do rockets go?   31
When is a shuttle like a glider?   31

Why do astronauts float
    in space?   32
Where do astronauts go to sleep? 33
Why do astronauts wear
    spacesuits?   33

Are there robots in space?   34
Which probe has travelled the
    furthest?   35
Have probes been to Mars?   35

Quiz time   36

Which star keeps us warm?

The Sun does. It is a star like all the others in the night sky, but it is much closer to Earth. The Sun is a giant ball of hot, glowing gas and it gives off heat that keeps the Earth warm. It also gives us light.

Hot hot hot!

The Sun's surface is so hot that it would melt a metal spacecraft flying near it! It is 15 times hotter than boiling water.

When is it night time during the day?

Sometimes the Sun, the Earth and the Moon all line up in space. When this happens, the Moon's shadow falls on the Earth, making it dark even if it's daytime. This is called an eclipse.

Eclipse

Sunspot

Why is the Sun spotty?

Some parts of the Sun's surface are cooler than the rest of it. These cooler parts appear darker than the rest of the Sun, like spots on its surface. They are called sunspots.

Remember

Never look straight at the Sun. Your eyes could be badly damaged.

Is Earth the only planet near the Sun?

No, there are other planets near the Sun. Mercury and Venus are nearer to the Sun than the Earth is. The other planets are further away. All the planets move around the Sun in huge circles. The Sun and its family of planets is called the Solar System.

Saturn

Uranus

Neptune

Pluto
(dwarf planet)

Draw

Can you draw a picture of all the planets? You could copy the pictures on this page.

Do other planets have moons?

Earth is not the only planet with a moon. Mars has two moons. Jupiter and Saturn have more than 30 moons each. Venus and Mercury are the only planets with no moons.

The Sun

Mercury

The Moon

Venus

Earth

Mars

Jupiter

What are the other planets like?

Mercury, Venus and Mars are rocky planets, like the Earth. They have solid surfaces. Jupiter, Saturn, Uranus and Neptune are balls of gas and liquid. They are much bigger than the rocky planets. Pluto is a dwarf planet.

One big, happy family!

There are millions of smaller members in the Sun's family. Tiny specks of dust speed between the planets along with chunks of rock called asteroids.

What is inside the Earth?

Crust

Mantle

Inner core

Outer core

There are layers of hot rock inside the Earth. We live on the Earth's surface where the rock is solid. Beneath the surface, the rock is hot. In some places, it has melted. This melted rock may leak from a volcano.

Living it up!

Earth is the only planet with water on its surface. This means that people, plants and animals can live here. No life has yet been found on other planets.

New Moon

Crescent Moon

First quarter Moon

Gibbous Moon

Full Moon

Why does the Moon change shape?

The Sun lights up one side of the Moon. The other side is dark. As the Moon circles the Earth, we see different parts of the lit side. This is why the Moon seems to change shape.

The Moon

Why do we have day and night?

The Earth spins round once every day. When the part you live on faces the Sun, it is daytime. When this part faces away from the Sun, the sunlight can't reach you. Then it is night time.

Look

Look at the picture of the Moon. The circles are called craters. They were made by lumps of rock smashing into the Moon's surface.

What is the hottest planet?

Venus is the hottest planet in the Solar System. Its surface is hotter than the inside of an oven. Venus is covered in a blanket of thick, yellow gas. The gases trap heat from the Sun but don't let it escape. This means that Venus can't cool down.

Back in a year!

Nobody has ever been to Mars. It is so far away that it would take a spacecraft six months to get there. It would take another six months to get home again!

Venus

Why is Mars called the red planet?

Mars looks red because it is covered with red rocks and red dust, the colour of rust. Sometimes, winds pick up the dust and make swirling dust storms. In 1971 dust storms covered the whole planet. The surface completely disappeared from view!

Mars

Which planet has the biggest volcano?

Mars has the biggest volcano. It is called Olympus Mons and it is three times higher than Mount Everest, the highest mountain on Earth. Olympus Mons has gently sloping sides, like an upside-down plate. Mars has many other volcanoes, too. There are also giant canyons and craters.

Discover

Try looking for Venus in the night sky. It looks like a bright star in the early morning or evening.

Does Pluto have its own moon?

Yes, it does. Pluto, a dwarf planet, has its own moon called Charon. Charon is half the size of Pluto and was discovered by scientists in 1978. It takes Charon six and a half Earth days to orbit around Pluto.

Charon, Pluto's moon

Pluto

Pluto's surface

Why does Mercury look like the Moon?

Mercury looks a bit like our Moon. It is covered in dents called craters. These were made when rocks crashed into the surface. There is no wind or rain on Mercury, or the Moon, to wear away the craters.

Sun trap!

Mercury is very close to the Sun. It gets much hotter there than on Earth. If you travelled to Mercury, you would need a special spacesuit and shoes to protect you from the heat.

← Mercury

Think

Pluto is really cold. Can you think why?

Which planet is baking hot and freezing cold?

Mercury is hot and cold. It spins very slowly. The side that faces the Sun is baked until it is hotter than the inside of an oven. When this side faces away from the Sun, it cools down until it is colder than a freezer.

What is the biggest planet?

Jupiter is the biggest planet. It is 11 times as wide as the Earth. All the other planets in the Solar System would fit inside it! Jupiter is covered in swirls of red and orange gas. These are giant storms.

Giant storm

Jupiter

Moon pizza!

Io is one of Jupiter's moons. It is covered in yellow and orange blotches. Io looks like a pizza in space! The blotches are made by hot liquid that comes out of volcanoes.

Saturn's rings

Saturn

Which planet has rings?

Saturn is surrounded by rings that shine brightly in the sunlight. The rings are made from millions and millions of lumps of ice. Some lumps are the size of ice cubes. Others are as big as cars!

Count

Can you count how many planet Earths there are on these pages?

Is there a giant made of gas?

Not really! However, Jupiter and Saturn are called gas giants. This is because they don't have solid surfaces like the Earth. They have a thick layer of gas and then liquid. You couldn't land on them in a spacecraft.

Which planet rolls around?

Uranus is different to the other planets. Most planets are almost upright. They spin as they move around the Sun. Uranus is tipped right over on its side. This planet spins, too, but it looks as though it is rolling around!

New new moons!

Astronomers (scientists that study space) keep finding new moons around Uranus. They have found 27 so far. There are four big moons and lots of small ones. But there may be more!

Uranus

Why does Neptune look so blue?

Neptune is covered in bright blue clouds. Sometimes there are streaky, icy white clouds, too. One white cloud is called The Scooter because it scoots around Neptune at high speed. There is also a giant storm called the Great Dark Spot.

Great Dark Spot

Neptune

Why do Neptune and Pluto swap places?

Most of the planets move around the Sun in huge circles. Pluto's circle is a bit squashed. This means that it is sometimes closer to the Sun than Neptune. Then it is Neptune's turn to be the planet that is furthest from the Sun!

Remember
Uranus and Neptune have rings. Which other two planets have rings, too?

Are there snowballs in space?

Not really! However, comets are a bit like giant snowballs. They are made up of dust and ice mixed together. When a comet gets close to the Sun, the ice begins to melt. Then dust and gas stream away from the comet. They form a long, bright tail.

What is a shooting star?

A shooting star is a bright streak across the night sky. It is not really a star. It is made when a small lump of rock shoots into the air above the Earth. Because the rock is going so fast, it burns brightly.

Comet

Asteroid belt

Does the Sun have a belt?

The Sun has a belt made up of lumps of rock called asteroids. We call this the asteroid belt. The asteroids move around the Sun between Mars and Jupiter. The biggest asteroids are round, but most are shaped like giant potatoes.

Discover
Can you find out the name of a famous comet?

How are stars made?

Stars are made from huge clouds of dust and gas. Gradually the cloud shrinks and all the gas and dust clump together. The centre of the cloud gets hotter and hotter and a new star begins to shine. The star gives off heat and light.

1. Cloud of gas and dust

3. Star begins to shine

4. New star

Shine on!

Stars can shine for thousands of millions of years! The Sun started shining five thousand million years ago. It will stop shining in another five thousand million years.

What is a group of stars called?

A group of stars is called a star cluster. A star cluster is made from a giant cloud of gas and dust. Some clusters contain just a few stars. Others contain hundreds of stars and they look like a big ball of light.

2. The cloud begins to spin

Star cluster

Are all stars white?

Only the most giant stars shine with a bright white light. This is because they are extremely hot. Smaller stars, such as our Sun, are not so hot. They look yellow instead. Very small stars are cooler still. They look red or brown.

Draw
Can you paint white, yellow and red stars on a sheet of black paper?

What is the Milky Way?

The stars in space are in huge groups called galaxies. Our galaxy is called the Milky Way. All the stars in the night sky are in the Milky Way. There are so many that you couldn't count them all in your whole lifetime!

Can galaxies crash?

Sometimes two galaxies crash into each other. But there is no giant bump. This is because galaxies are mostly made of empty space! The stars just go past each other. Galaxies can pull each other out of shape.

Count

Look at the pictures on these pages. How many different shapes of galaxies can you find?

The Milky Way

Elliptical
galaxy

Do galaxies have arms?

Some galaxies have arms that curl in a spiral, like the Milky Way. Other galaxies, called elliptical galaxies, have a round, squashed shape. Many galaxies have no shape and are called irregular galaxies.

Irregular
galaxy

Great galaxies!

There are thousands of millions of galaxies in space. Some are much smaller than the Milky Way. Others are much larger. They all contain too many stars to count!

Spiral
galaxy

How does a shuttle get into space?

Booster rocket

Tower

A shuttle blasts into space like a big rocket. It has rocket motors in its tail. They get fuel from a giant fuel tank. There are two booster rockets, too. The fuel tank and the booster rockets fall off before the shuttle reaches space.

USA

Rocket power!

Rockets are filled with fuel. The fuel burns in the rocket motor to make hot gases. The gases rush out of the motor and push the rocket upwards.

Fuel
tank

Space
shuttle

Rocket
motors

How fast do rockets go?

Very, very fast indeed! After blasting off, a rocket goes faster and faster and higher and higher. When it reaches space, it is going 30 times faster than a jumbo jet. If a rocket went slower than this it would fall back to Earth.

Rocket

Make

Blow up a balloon and then let it go. The air rushes out and pushes the balloon along, like a simple rocket.

When is a shuttle like a glider?

When a shuttle travels back to Earth it slows down. Then it begins to fall. It does not use its motors to fly down. Instead, it flies like a giant glider. The shuttle lands on a long runway and uses a parachute to slow to a stop.

Why do astronauts float in space?

When things are in space they don't have any weight. This means everything floats. So do astronauts! This makes them feel sick, too. In a spacecraft everything is fixed down to stop it floating away. Astronauts have footholds and handholds to grab onto.

All packed?

Astronauts must take everything they need into space. In space there is no air, water or food. All of these things have to be packed into the spacecraft and taken into space.

Astronaut

Sleeping bag

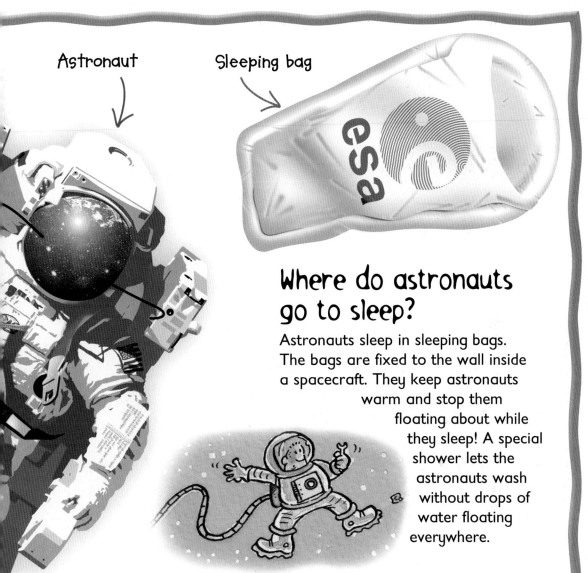

esa

Where do astronauts go to sleep?

Astronauts sleep in sleeping bags. The bags are fixed to the wall inside a spacecraft. They keep astronauts warm and stop them floating about while they sleep! A special shower lets the astronauts wash without drops of water floating everywhere.

Why do astronauts wear spacesuits?

Space is a dangerous place. Spacesuits protect astronauts when they go outside their spacecraft. There is no air in space. So a spacesuit has a supply of air for the astronaut to breathe. The suit also stops an astronaut from getting too hot or too cold.

Remember

Can you remember why astronauts have to carry air with them in space?

Are there robots in space?

There are robot spacecraft, called probes, in space. They have visited all the planets. Some probes travel around the planets. They send photographs and other information back to Earth. Other probes land on a planet to take a closer look.

Snap happy!
A probe called *Voyager 2* was the first to visit Uranus and Neptune. It took photographs of the planets and sent them back to Earth.

Viking probe on Mars

Voyager 1

Jupiter

Which probe has travelled the furthest?

A probe called *Voyager 1* was launched from Earth in 1977. It visited Jupiter in 1979 and then Saturn in 1980. Then it kept going, out of the Solar System. *Voyager 1* is now 14 thousand million kilometres from Earth!

Draw

Try designing your own robot explorer. You can take some ideas from these pages.

Sojourner

Have probes been to Mars?

More probes have been to Mars than any other planet. In 1997 a probe called Pathfinder landed on Mars. Inside Pathfinder was a tiny robot vehicle, called *Sojourner*. Scientists steered it using remote control. It investigated the soil and rocks on Mars.

Quiz time

Do you remember what you have read about space?
Here are some questions to test your memory. The pictures will help you. If you get stuck, read the pages again.

1. Which star keeps us warm?

page 10

2. Why is the Sun spotty?

page 11

page 16

3. What is the hottest planet?

4. Why is Mars called the red planet?

page 17

5. What is Charon?

page 18

6. What is a shooting star?

page 24

7. Does the Sun have a belt?

page 25

11. How does a shuttle get into space?

page 30

8. What is a group of stars called?

page 27

12. When is a shuttle like a glider?

page 31

13. Why do astronauts float in space?

page 32

9. What is the Milky Way?

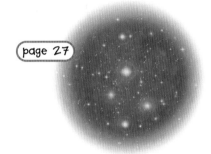

page 28

10. Can galaxies crash?

page 28

37

Questions about...

Where did the Earth come from?	40
Why does the Moon look lumpy?	40
What is the Earth made of?	41
Why does the Earth spin?	42
Why do we have day and night?	43
Do people live on the Moon?	43

What is a fossil?	46
How is a fossil made?	47
Why do rocks crumble?	47
What is a volcano?	48
What is a range?	49
How are mountains made?	49
Why are there earthquakes?	50
What is the Richter Scale?	51
Can earthquakes start fires?	51

What is inside the Earth?	44
Can we travel into the Earth?	45
Does the ground move?	45

What is a glacier?	52
Can ice be fun?	53
What is an iceberg?	53

Planet Earth

Where do rivers flow to?	54
Why are there waterfalls?	54
What is a lake?	55

Are there mountains under. the sea?	56
Why do coasts change?	57
What is coral?	57
How are caves made?	58
Can lava make caves?	59
What is a stalactite?	59

Is there water in the desert?	60
What are grasslands?	60
What is a rainforest?	61
Where does rain come from?	62
How does a tornado start?	63
Do storms have eyes?	63

How do we damage the Earth?	64
What is recycling?	65
How can we protect the Earth?	65

Quiz time	66

Where did the Earth come from?

The Earth came from a cloud of dust. The dust whizzed around the Sun at speed and and began to stick together to form lumps of rock. The rocks crashed into each other to make the planets. The Earth is one of these planets.

A cloud of dust spun around the Sun

Why does the Moon look lumpy?

Big rocks from space, called meteorites, have crashed into the Moon and made dents on its surface. These dents are called craters and they give the Moon a lumpy appearance.

Lumps of rock began to form

Look

At night, use some binoculars to look at the Moon. Can you see craters on its surface?

The Earth was formed from the lumps of rock →

What is the Earth made of?

The Earth is a huge ball-shaped lump of rock. Most of the Earth's surface is covered by water – this makes the seas and oceans. Rock that is not covered by water makes the land.

Face the Moon!

The Moon travels around the Earth. As the Moon doesn't spin, we only ever see one side of its surface.

41

Why does the Earth spin?

Morning

The Earth is always spinning. This is because it was made from a spinning cloud of gas and dust. As it spins, the Earth leans a little to one side. It takes the Earth 24 hours to spin around once. This period of time is called a day.

Evening

Discover
There are 24 hours in a day. How many minutes are there in one hour?

Spinning Earth

Hot and cold!

In the Caribbean, the sea can be as warm as a bath. In the Arctic, it is so cold, that the sea freezes over.

Why do we have day and night?

Every day, each part of the Earth spins towards the Sun, and then away from it. When a part of the Earth is facing the Sun, it is daytime there. When that part is facing away from Earth, it is night time.

Mid-day

The Sun

Night

Do people live on the Moon?

No they don't. There is no air on the Moon so people cannot live there. Astronauts have visited the Moon in space rockets. They wear special equipment to help them breathe.

What is inside the Earth?

There are different layers inside the Earth. There is a thin, rocky crust, a solid area called the mantle and a centre called the core. The outer part of the core is made of hot, liquid metal. The inner core is made of solid metal.

Natural magnet!

Near the centre of the Earth is hot, liquid iron. As the Earth spins, the iron behaves like a magnet. This is why a compass needle points to North and South.

Can we travel into the Earth?

No, we can't. The Earth's core is incredibly hot and so far down that no one could ever go there. Sometimes, boiling-hot liquid rock bursts up through the Earth's surface from mountains called volcanoes.

Inner core

Outer core

Mantle

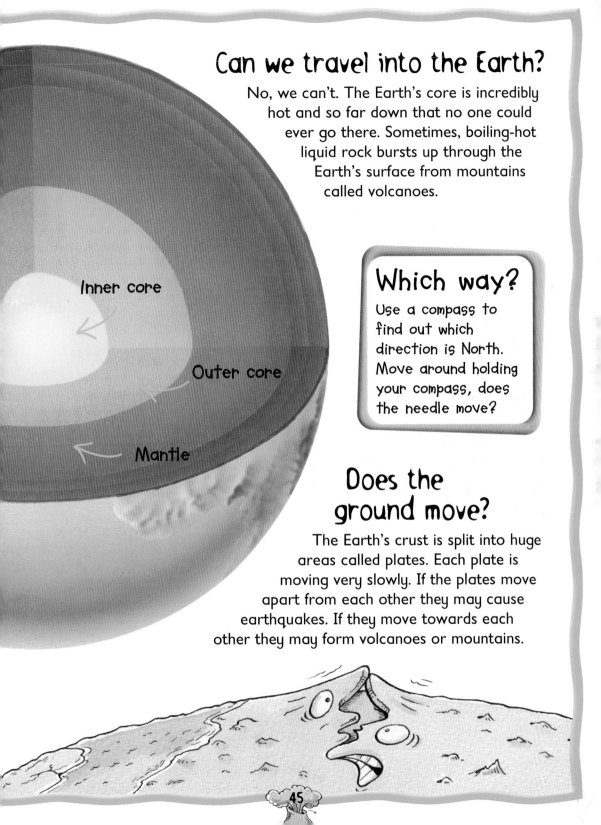

Which way?

Use a compass to find out which direction is North. Move around holding your compass, does the needle move?

Does the ground move?

The Earth's crust is split into huge areas called plates. Each plate is moving very slowly. If the plates move apart from each other they may cause earthquakes. If they move towards each other they may form volcanoes or mountains.

What is a fossil?

A trilobite was an ancient sea creature

A fossil was once a living thing that has now turned to stone. By studying fossils, scientists can learn more about the past and how animals, such as dinosaurs, used to live.

Scientists digging up and studying fossils

How is a fossil made?

It takes millions of years to make a fossil. When an animal dies, it may be buried by sand. The soft parts of its body rot away, leaving just bones, teeth or shells. These slowly turn to rock and a fossil has formed.

Find

Look for rocks in your garden. They may be so old dinosaurs could have trodden on them.

1. The trilobite dies

2. The trilobite gets covered with mud

3. The mud turns to stone

House of stones!

In Turkey, some people live in caves. These huge cone-shaped rocks stay very cool in the hot weather.

4. The fossil forms inside the stone

Why do rocks crumble?

When a rock is warmed up by the Sun it gets a little bigger. When it cools down, the rock shrinks to its original size. If this process happens to a rock too often, it starts to crumble away.

What is a volcano?

A volcano is a mountain that sometimes shoots hot, liquid rock out of its top. Deep inside a volcano is an area called a magma chamber. This is filled with liquid rock. If pressure builds up in the chamber, the volcano may explode, and liquid rock will shoot out of the top.

Erupting volcano

Liquid rock

Magma chamber

What is a range?

A range is the name for a group of mountains. The biggest ranges are the Alps in Europe, the Andes in South America, the Rockies in North America and the highest of all – the Himalayas in Asia.

How are mountains made?

One way that mountains are formed is when the Earth's plates crash together. The crust at the edge of the plates slowly crumples and folds. Over millions of years this pushes up mountains. The Himalayan Mountains in Asia were made this way.

Mountain range is pushed up

Layer on layer

When a volcano erupts, the hot lava cools and forms a rocky layer. With each new eruption, another layer is added and the volcano gets bigger.

Why are there earthquakes?

Earthquakes happen when the plates in the Earth's crust move apart suddenly, or rub together. They start deep underground in an area called the focus. The land above the focus is shaken violently. The worst part of the earthquake happens above the focus, in an area called the epicentre.

Epicentre

Remember

Can you remember what breaks at level 5 on the Richter Scale? Read these pages again to refresh your memory.

Focus

Lights swing at level 3

Windows break at level 5

Bridges and buildings collapse at level 7

What is The Richter Scale?

The Richter Scale measures the strength of an earthquake. It starts at number one and goes up to number eight. The higher the number, the more powerful and destructive the earthquake.

Super senses!

Some people believe that animals can sense when an earthquake is about to happen!

Can earthquakes start fires?

Yes, a powerful earthquake can cause fires. In 1906, a huge earthquake in San Francisco, USA caused lots of fires. The fires burnt down most of the city and the people who lived there became homeless.

What is a glacier?

Glaciers are huge rivers of ice found near the tops of mountains. Snow falls on the mountain and becomes squashed to make ice. The ice forms a glacier that slowly moves down the mountainside until it melts.

Moving glacier

Fancy flakes!

Snowflakes are made of millions of tiny crystals. No two snowflakes are the same because the crystals make millions of different shapes.

Melted ice

Can ice be fun?

Yes, it can! Many people go ice skating and they wear special boots with blades on them called ice skates. Figure skaters are skilled athletes who compete to win prizes.

What is an iceberg?

Icebergs are big chunks of ice that have broken off glaciers and drifted into the sea. Only a small part of the iceberg can be seen above the water. The main part of the iceberg is hidden under the water.

Iceberg

Look

Next time it snows, put some gloves on and let the snowflakes fall into your hand. Can you see crystals?

Where do rivers flow to?

Rivers flow to the sea or into lakes. They start off as small streams in hills and mountains. The streams flow downhill, getting bigger and wider. The place where a river meets the sea, or flows into a lake, is called the river mouth.

Oxbow lake

River mouth

Why are there waterfalls?

Waterfalls are made when water wears down rocks to make a cliff face. The water then falls over the edge into a deep pool called a plunge pool. Waterfalls may only be a few centimetres high, or several hundred metres high!

Discover

Try to find out the name of the highest waterfall in the world. Where is it?

A river begins in the mountains

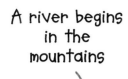

Meander

Risky business!

Salmon are a type of fish. Every year, fishermen try to catch them as they swim back to the river they were born in to have their babies.

What is a lake?

A lake is a big area of water that is surrounded by land. Some lakes are so big that they are called inland seas. Most lake water is fresh rather than salty. The biggest lake in the world is the Caspian Sea in Asia.

Lake

Are there mountains under the sea?

Ocean

Yes there are. Mountains lie hidden in very deep oceans. The ocean floor is very flat and is called a plain. Large mountain ranges may rise across the plain. Some oceans even have underwater volcanoes.

Exploring underwater!

Scientists can learn more about life underwater by exploring the ocean in submarines. They can be underwater for months at a time.

Why do coasts change?

The coast is where the land meets the sea, and it is always changing. In many places, waves crash onto land and rocks, slowly breaking them up. This can change the shape of the coastline.

Coastline

Plain

Underwater volcano

Trench

Find out

Have a look in an atlas to find out which ocean you live closest to.

What is coral?

Coral is made from polyps. These are tiny creatures the size of pin heads that live in warm, shallow waters. The polyps join together in large groups and create rocky homes. These are called coral reefs.

How are caves made?

When rain falls on rock, it can make caves. Rainwater mixes with a gas in the air called carbon dioxide. This makes a strong acid. This acid can attack the rock and make it disappear. Underground, the rainwater makes caves in which streams and lakes can be found.

Underground cave

Lava cave

Remember

Stalactites hold on tight, stalagmites might reach the top!

Can lava make caves?

When a volcano erupts and lava flows through the mountain, it can carve out a cave. A long time after the eruption, when the volcano is no longer active, people can walk through this lava cave without having to bend down.

What is a stalactite?

Rocky spikes that hang from cave ceilings are called stalactites. When water drips from the cave ceiling, it leaves tiny amounts of a rocky substance behind. Very slowly, over a long period of time, this grows into a stalactite.

Super spiky!

Stalagmites grow up from the cave floor. Dripping water leaves a rocky substance that grows into a rocky spike.

Is there water in the desert?

Yes there is. Deserts sometimes get rain. This rainwater seeps into the sand and collects in rock. The water then builds up and forms a pool called an oasis. Plants grow around the oasis and animals visit the pool to drink.

Oasis

What are grasslands?

Grasslands are found when there is too much rain for a desert but not enough rain for a forest. Large numbers of animals can be found living and feeding on grasslands, including zebras, antelopes and lions.

Draw

Create a picture of a camel crossing a desert – don't forget to include its wide feet!

Big feet!

Camels have wide feet that stop them sinking into the sand. They can also store water in their bodies for a long time.

Rainforest

What is a rainforest?

In hot places, such as South America, grow areas of thick, green forest. These are rainforests, and they are home to many amazing plants and animals. Rainforests have rainy weather all year round.

Where does rain come from?

Rain comes from the ocean! Water moves between the ocean, air and land in a water cycle. A fine mist of water rises into the air from the ocean and from plants. This fine mist then forms clouds. Water can fall from the clouds as rain.

Water falls from clouds as rain

Water cycle

Stormy weather!

Every day there are more than 45,000 thunderstorms on the Earth! Thunderstorms are most common in tropical places, such as Indonesia.

How does a tornado start?

A tornado is the fastest wind on Earth. Tornadoes
start over very hot ground. Here, warm air rises
quickly and makes a spinning funnel. This funnel
acts like a vacuum cleaner, destroying buildings
and lifting cars and lorries off the ground.

Tornado

A fine mist of
water rises from
the ocean

Do storms have eyes?

Yes, storms do have eyes! A hurricane is a very
dangerous storm. The centre of a hurricane is
called the eye and here it is completely still.
However, the rest of the storm can reach
speeds of up to 300 kilometres an hour.

How do we damage the Earth?

Some of the things that people do can damage the Earth. Factories pump chemicals into the air and water. Forests are being cut down, killing the wildlife that lives there, and fumes from cars are clogging up the air. Scientists are trying to find new ways to protect the Earth before it is too late.

Help

Save all of your empty drinks cans and bottles and take them to your recycling centre.

Fumes from factories

Rubbish dumped in rivers

Traffic fumes

Save the planet!

Large areas of land have been made into national parks where wildlife is protected. People can go there to learn about both plants and animals.

1. Old bottles are collected from bottle banks

What is recycling?

Recycling is when people collect waste materials such as paper and plastic. The waste is then taken to a recycling centre and changed back into useful materials to make many of the things we use today.

2. The glass or plastic are re-cycled to make raw materials

Trees are cut down

3. The raw materials are re-used to make new bottles

How can we protect the Earth?

There are lots of things we can do to protect our planet. Recycling, picking up litter, switching lights off and walking to the shops all help to make a difference.

Quiz time

3. What is inside the Earth?

page 44

Do you remember what you have read about planet Earth? These questions will test your memory. The pictures will help you. If you get stuck, read the pages again.

4. What is a fossil?

page 46

page 40

1. Why does the Moon look lumpy?

5. What is a range?

page 49

6. Can earthquakes start fires?

page 51

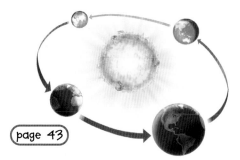

page 43

2. Why do we have day and night?

7. Can ice be fun?

page 53

page 53

8. What is an iceberg?

page 54

9. Why are there waterfalls?

page 59

10. Can lava make caves?

page 59

11. What is a stalactite?

page 61

12. What is a rainforest?

page 63

13. Do storms have eyes?

Answers

1. Because there are craters on its surface
2. Because the Earth is always spinning
3. Lots of different layers of rocks
4. A living thing that has turned to stone
5. A group of mountains
6. Yes, they can
7. Yes, people skate on ice for fun
8. A big chunk of ice that has broken off a glacier
9. Because water flows over cliffs
10. Yes it can
11. A rocky spike that hangs from the ceiling of a cave
12. A large, thick, green forest that grows in a hot place
13. Yes, the centre of a hurricane is called the eye

Questions about...

Is there only one big ocean? 70
Are there mountains under
   the sea? 71
Where do islands come from? 71

Do seashells have feet? 72
Can starfish grow arms? 72
When is a sponge like an animal? 73

What is the scariest shark? 76
Do some sharks use hammers? 77
When is a shark like a pup? 77

Who builds walls beneath the sea? 78
How do fish keep clean? 79
When is a fish like a clown? 79

Are there schools in the sea? 74
Which fish looks like an oar? 75
Do fish like to sunbathe? 75

What is the biggest sea animal? 80
Can whales sing songs? 81
Do whales grow tusks? 81

Do lions live in the sea? 82
Who sleeps in seaweed? 83
Can a walrus change colour? 83

Are there crocodiles in the sea? 84
Which lizard loves to swim? 85
How deep can a turtle dive? 85

Oceans

Can seabirds sleep as they fly?   86
Do seabirds dig burrows?   87
Which bird dives for its dinner?   87

How do polar bears learn
    to swim?   88
Are penguins fast swimmers?   89
Which penguin dad likes
    to babysit?   89

Is seaweed good to eat?   90
How are lobsters caught?   91
Do pearls grow at sea?   91

Are there chimneys under
    the sea?   92
Do monsters live in the sea?   93
What is a mermaid?   93

How do divers breathe
    underwater?   94
Can people ride the waves?   95
What is a jetski?   95

Quiz time   96

Is there only one big ocean?

It seems that way. All the oceans flow into each other, but we know them as four different oceans – the Pacific, Atlantic, Indian and Arctic. The land we live on, the continents, rises out of the oceans. More than two-thirds of the Earth's rocky surface is covered by oceans.

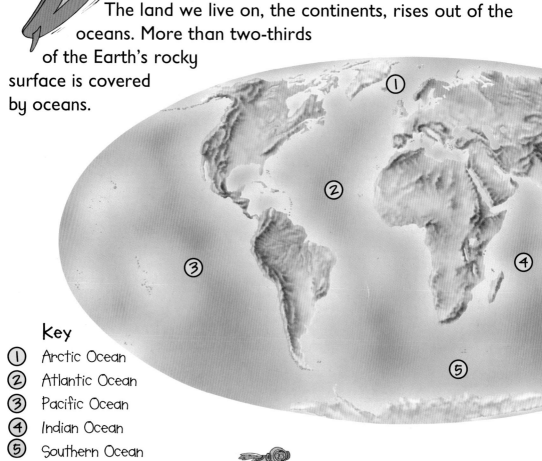

Key

① Arctic Ocean
② Atlantic Ocean
③ Pacific Ocean
④ Indian Ocean
⑤ Southern Ocean

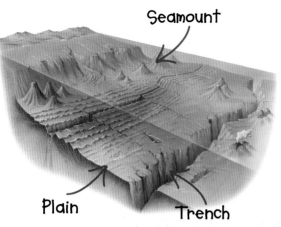

Seamount

Plain

Trench

Are there mountains under the sea?

Yes there are. The land beneath the sea is covered by mountains, flat areas called plains and deep valleys called trenches. There are also huge underwater volcanoes called seamounts.

Salty or fresh!

Almost all of the world's water is in the oceans. Only a tiny amount is in freshwater lakes and rivers.

Were do islands come from?

Islands are 'born' beneath the sea. If an underwater volcano erupts, it throws out hot, sticky lava. This cools and hardens in the water. Layers of lava build up and up, until a new island peeps above the waves.

Look

Look at the world map to find where you live. Which ocean is nearest to you?

Do seashells have feet?

Tiny animals called limpets live inside some seashells.
They stick to rocks at the shoreline where they eat slimy, green plants called algae. When the tide is out, limpets stick to the rocks like glue, with a strong muscular foot. They only move when the tide crashes in.

Can starfish grow arms?

Yes they can. Starfish may have as many as 40 arms, called rays. If a hungry crab grabs hold of one, the starfish abandons its arm, and uses the others to make its getaway. It then begins to grow a new arm.

Limpets

Anemone

Starfish

Fighting fit!

Anemones are a kind of sea-living plant. Some anemones fight over their feeding grounds. Beadlet anemones shoot sharp, tiny hooks at each other until the weakest one gives in.

When is a sponge like an animal?

Sponges are animals! They are very simple creatures that filter food from sea water. The natural sponge that you use in the bath is a long-dead dried-out sponge!

Crab

Sponge

Find

When you next visit a beach, try to find a rockpool. Write a list of what you see.

Are there schools in the sea?

Some fish live in big groups called schools. This may protect them from hungry hunters. There are thousands of different types of fish in the sea. Most are covered in shiny scales and use fins and tails to swim. Fish have gills that take in oxygen from the water so that they can breathe.

Read

What is a big group of fish called? Read this page to find out.

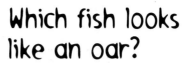

Which fish looks like an oar?

The oarfish does – and it can grow to be as long as four canoes! It is the longest bony fish and is found in all the world's oceans. Oarfish have a bright red fin along the length of their back. They swim upright through the water.

Oarfish

Flying high!

Flying fish cannot really fly. Fish can't survive out of water, but flying fish sometimes leap above the waves when they are swimming at high speed. They use their long fins to glide through the air for as long as 30 seconds.

Do fish like to sunbathe?

Sunfish like sunbathing. Ocean sunfish are huge fish that can weigh as much as one tonne – as heavy as a small car! They like to swim at the surface of the water, as if they're sunbathing.

School of fish

What is the scariest shark?

Great whites are the scariest sharks.
These huge fish speed through the
water at 30 kilometres an
hour. Unlike most fish, the
great white shark has warm blood. This allows
its muscles to work well but it also means that
it needs to eat lots of meat. Great white
sharks are fierce hunters. They will
attack and eat almost anything, but
prefer to feed on seals.

Great white shark

Draw
Using felt—tip
pens, draw your
own underwater
picture. Include a
great white shark.

Do some sharks use hammers?

Not really! Hammerhead sharks have hammer-shaped heads to search for food. With a nostril and an eye on each end of the 'hammer', they swing their heads from side to side, looking for a meal.

Hammerhead shark

Yum yum!

Most sharks are meat eaters. Herring are a favourite food for sand tiger and thresher sharks, while a hungry tiger shark will gobble up just about anything!

When is a shark like a pup?

When it's a baby. Young sharks are called pups. Some grow inside their mother's body. Others hatch from eggs straight into the sea.

Who builds walls beneath the sea?

Tiny animals build underwater walls. These walls are made of coral, the leftover skeletons of tiny sea animals called polyps. Over millions of years, enough skeletons pile up to form walls. These make a coral reef. All kinds of creatures live around a reef.

Seahorse

Parrot fish

Look
Do you know where the Great Barrier Reef is? Look in an atlas to find out.

Clownfish

How do fish keep clean?

Cleaner wrasse are little fish that help other fish to keep clean! Larger fish, such as groupers and moray eels, visit the cleaner wrasse, which nibbles all the bugs and bits of dirt off the bigger fishes' bodies – what a feast!

Super reef

You can see the Great Barrier Reef from space! At over 2000 kilometres long, it is the largest thing ever built by living creatures.

Coral reef

Lionfish

Cleaner wrasse fish

Sea anemone

When is a fish like a clown?

When it's a clownfish. These fish are brightly coloured, like circus clowns. They live among the stinging arms (tentacles) of the sea anemone. Clownfish swim among the stingers, where they are safe from enemies.

What is the biggest sea animal?

The blue whale is the biggest animal in the ocean – and the whole planet. It is about 30 metres long and can weigh up to 150 tonnes. It feeds on tiny, shrimp-like creatures called krill – and eats about four tonnes every day! Like other great whales, the blue whale has special, sieve-like parts in its mouth that are called baleen plates.

Blue whale

Can whales sing songs?

All whales make sounds, such as squeaks and moans. The humpback whale really does seem to sing. The males probably do this to attract a mate. He may repeat his song for up to 20 hours!

Humpback whale

Stick around!

Barnacles are shellfish. They attach themselves to ships, or the bodies of grey whales and other large sea animals.

Measure

The blue whale is 30 metres long. Can you measure how long you are?

Do whales grow tusks?

The narwhal has a tusk like a unicorn's. This tusk is a long, twirly tooth that comes out of the whale's head. The males use their tusks as weapons when they fight over females. The tusk can grow to 3 metres in length.

Do lions live in the sea?

There are lions in the sea, but not the furry, roaring kind. Sea lions, seals and walruses are all warm-blooded animals that have adapted to ocean life. They have flippers instead of legs – far more useful for swimming. A thick layer of fat under the skin keeps them warm in cold water.

Seal

Think
What do you think whales, dolphins and seals have in common with humans?

Who sleeps in seaweed?

Sea otters do! They live in forests of giant seaweed, called kelp. When they sleep, they wrap strands of kelp around their bodies to stop themselves being washed out to sea.

Sea otter

Sea lion

Singing seal!

Leopard seals sing in their sleep! These seals, found in the Antarctic, chirp and whistle while they snooze.

Can a walrus change colour?

Walruses seem to change colour. In cold water, a walrus can look pale brown or even white. This is because blood drains from the skin to stop the body losing heat. On land, blood returns to the skin and the walrus looks pink!

Are there crocodiles in the sea?

Most crocodiles live in rivers and swamps. The saltwater crocodile also swims out to sea – it doesn't seem to mind the salty water. These crocodiles are huge, and can grow to be 7 metres long and one tonne in weight.

Saltwater crocodile

Find out

Turtles only come ashore for one reason. Can you find out why?

Which lizard loves to swim?

Most lizards live on land, where it is easier to warm up their cold-blooded bodies. Marine iguanas depend on the sea for food. They dive underwater to eat seaweed growing on rocks. When they are not diving, they sit on rocks and soak up the sunshine.

How deep can a turtle dive?

Leatherback turtles can dive up to 1200 metres for their dinner. They are the biggest sea turtles and they make the deepest dives. Leatherbacks feed mostly on jellyfish but also eat crabs, lobsters and starfish.

Leatherback turtle →

Slithery snakes!

There are poisonous snakes in the sea. The banded sea snake and the yellow-bellied sea snake both use poison to kill their prey. Their poison is far stronger than that of land snakes.

Can seabirds sleep as they fly?

Wandering albatrosses are the biggest seabirds and spend months at sea. They are such good gliders that they even sleep as they fly. To feed, they sit on the surface of the water, where they catch creatures such as squid. An albatross has a wingspan of around 3 metres – about the length of a family car!

Wandering albatross

Think

Seabirds have webbed feet. Why do you think this is? Do you have webbed feet?

Do seabirds dig burrows?

Most seabirds make nests on cliffs.
The puffin digs a burrow on the clifftop, like a
rabbit. Sometimes, a puffin even takes
over an empty rabbit hole. Here it lays
its egg. Both parents look after the
chick when it hatches.

Puffins

Dancing birds!

Boobies are a type of seabird that live in large groups. The males have bright red or blue feet. When they are looking for a mate, they dance in front of the female, trying to attract her with their colourful feet!

Which bird dives for its dinner?

The gannet dives headfirst into the ocean to catch fish in its beak. It dives at high-speed and hits the water hard. Luckily, the gannet is protected by cushions of air inside its head that absorb most of the shock.

How do polar bears learn to swim?

Polar bears are good swimmers and they live around the freezing Arctic Ocean. They learn to swim when they are cubs, by following their mother into the water. With their big front paws, the bears paddle through the water. They can swim for many hours.

Polar bears

Imagine
Pretend to be a penguin. Imagine what life is like at the South Pole.

Are penguins fast swimmers?

Penguins are birds – but they cannot fly. All penguins are fast swimmers. The fastest swimmer is the gentoo penguin. It can reach speeds of 27 kilometres an hour underwater.

Gentoo penguin

Small and tall!

The smallest penguin is the fairy penguin at just 40 centimetres tall. The biggest is the emperor penguin at 1.3 metres in height – as tall as a seven-year-old child!

Which penguin dad likes to babysit?

Emperor penguin dads look after the baby chicks. The female lays an egg and leaves her mate to keep it warm. The penguin dad balances the egg on his feet to keep it off the freezing ice. He goes without food until the chick hatches. When it does, the mother returns and both parents look after it.

Is seaweed good to eat?

Seaweed can be very good to eat. In shallow, warm seawater, people can grow their own seaweed. It is then dried in the sun, which helps to keep it fresh. Seaweed is even used to make ice cream!

Growing seaweed

List

Make a list of the things you can eat that come from the ocean. Which of these things have you eaten before?

How do we get salt from the sea?

Sea water is salty. Salt is an important substance. In hot, low-lying areas, people build walls to hold shallow pools of sea water. The water dries up in the sun, leaving behind crystals of salt.

How are lobsters caught?

Lobsters are large shellfish that are good to eat. Fishermen catch them in wooden cages called pots. The lobsters are attracted to dead fish placed in the pots. They push the door of the pot open to get to the fish, but once inside, the lobster can't get out again.

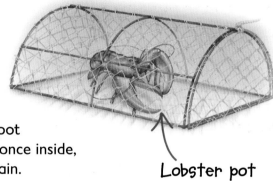

Lobster pot

Do pearls grow at sea?

Yes they do. Pearls grow inside oysters, a kind of shellfish. If a grain of sand gets stuck in an oyster's shell, it irritates its soft body. The oyster coats the grain with a substance that it uses to line the inside of its shell. In time, more coats are added and a pearl begins to form.

Are there chimneys under the sea?

Rocky chimneys on the ocean floor give off clouds of hot water. These chimneys lie deep beneath the ocean. The hot water feeds strange creatures such as tube worms and sea spiders.

Rat tail fish

Watery village!

In 1963, diver Jacques Cousteau built a village on the bed of the Red Sea. Along with four other divers, he lived there for a whole month.

Giant clams

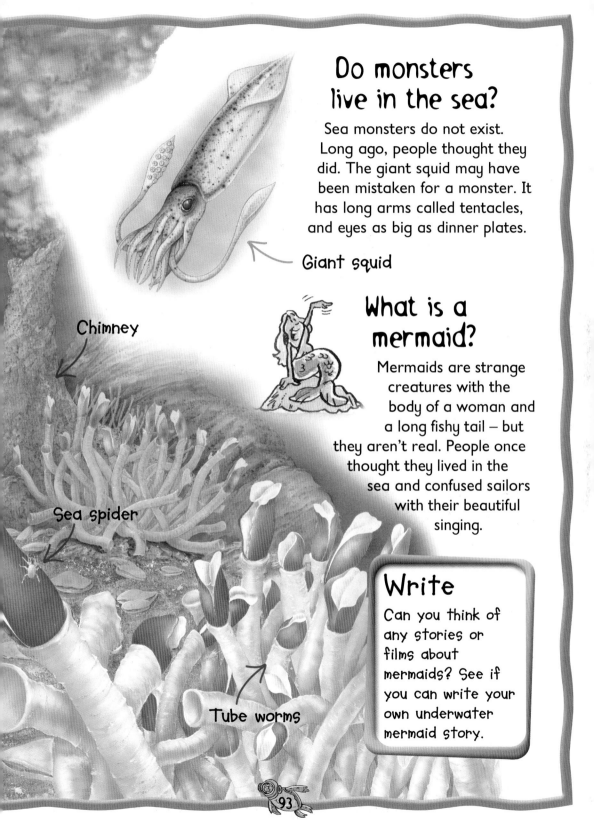

Do monsters live in the sea?

Sea monsters do not exist. Long ago, people thought they did. The giant squid may have been mistaken for a monster. It has long arms called tentacles, and eyes as big as dinner plates.

Giant squid

What is a mermaid?

Mermaids are strange creatures with the body of a woman and a long fishy tail — but they aren't real. People once thought they lived in the sea and confused sailors with their beautiful singing.

Chimney

Sea spider

Tube worms

Write

Can you think of any stories or films about mermaids? See if you can write your own underwater mermaid story.

How do divers breathe underwater?

Divers have a spare pair of lungs. Scuba divers carry a special piece of breathing equipment called an 'aqua lung'. These are tanks filled with oxygen (air) that sit on the divers' backs. A long tube supplies the diver with air.

Water record!

A single boat towed 100 waterskiers! This record was made off the coast of Australia in 1986 and no one has beaten it yet. The drag boat was a cruiser called 'Reef Cat'.

Can people ride the waves?

Yes they can, on surfboards. Surfing became popular in the 1950s. Modern surfboards are made of super-light material. People stand up on their boards and ride the waves. The best places to surf are off the coasts of Mexico and Hawaii.

Surfer

Aqua lung

Diver

Wear

Try wearing some goggles in the bath. What can you see?

What is a jetski?

A jetski is like a motorbike without wheels that travels on water. It pushes out a jet of water behind it, which pushes it forward. Some jetskiers can reach speeds of 100 kilometres an hour.

Quiz time

page 75

Do you remember what you have read about oceans? Here are some questions to test your memory. The pictures will help you. If you get stuck, read the pages again.

3. Which fish looks like an oar?

4. Do some sharks use hammers?

page 77

1. Are there mountains under the sea?

page 71

page 77

2. When is a sponge like an animal?

page 73

5. When is a shark like a pup?

page 83

6. Who sleeps in seaweed?

7. Are there crocodiles
in the sea?

page 84

11. Is seaweed
good to eat?

page 90

8. Can seabirds sleep
as they fly?

page 86

12. What is a
mermaid?

page 93

13. How do divers
breathe underwater?

page 94

9. How do polar bears
learn to swim?

page 88

10. Which penguin dad
likes to babysit?

page 89

Answers

1. Yes, there are
2. A sponge is an animal
3. The oarfish
4. No, but the hammerhead shark has a hammershaped head
5. When it's a baby – young sharks are called pups
6. The sea otter
7. The saltwater crocodile swims in the sea
8. Yes, the wandering albatross can
9. By following their mother into the water
10. The emperor penguin
11. Yes, it can be
12. A creature that is half–woman, half–fish
13. By using an aqua lung

Questions about...

Why is summer warm and sunny? 100
Why are days longer in summer? 100
Why do leaves fall in autumn? 101

What is the sunniest place? 102
When is a lake not a lake? 103
What happens when it
  doesn't rain? 103

Where does rain come from? 106
Are all clouds small and fluffy? 107
What rain never lands? 107

What happens in a flood? 108
Did Noah build an ark? 109
Can there be a flood in a desert? 109

What is snow made of? 110
When is snow dangerous? 111
Are all snowflakes the same? 111

Does Earth have a blanket? 104
Where does it rain every day? 104
How deep is the atmosphere? 105

Weather

Where are the fastest winds?   112
Which storm has an eye?   113
How do we measure wind?   113

What makes the sky clap?   114
When is lightning like a fork?   115
Does lightning hit buildings?   115

Which bird spins in the wind?   120
What is a weather house?   121
How do we know how hot it is?   121

Can planes tell the weather?   122
Why do scientists fly balloons?   123
How do we watch
    weather from space?   123

Did weather kill the dinosaurs?   124
Can trees affect the weather?   125
Is our weather changing?   125

What is a rainbow made of?   116
When does the sky have curtains?   117
When can you see three suns?   117

What is a rain dance?   118
Who first recorded the weather?   118
Are weather sayings true?   119

Quiz time   126

Why is summer warm and sunny?

The Earth is tipped to one side as it moves round the Sun. Some of the year, the north half of the Earth faces the Sun. Then the Sun is higher in the sky, making the weather warm. This is summer. When the southern half of the Earth faces the Sun, it is winter in the north.

Spring in the north

Summer in the north

The Sun

Why are days longer in summer?

Summer days are longer because the Earth is tilted and spins round. In summer, the Sun rises earlier and sets later. This makes daytime last longer than night. In the middle of summer in Sweden it is light for 21 hours!

Winter in
the north

Why do leaves fall in autumn?

Autumn comes between summer and winter.
Many trees lose their leaves in autumn
because it is hard for them to grow in the
dark winter months. The leaves turn from
green to red, orange or brown. Then they
fall to the ground.

Autumn in the north

Find

Can you find
photographs of red,
orange and brown
leaves in autumn?

Sunshine at midnight!

At the North and South
Poles, the Sun never sets in
summer. It is light all day. In
winter, the Sun never rises.
Then it is dark all day long!

What is the sunniest place?

The Sahara Desert in North Africa is the sunniest place on Earth. It is sunny for nearly 12 hours every day! It hardly rains, which makes it hard for plants and animals to live here. People dress in loose clothes to stop being sunburnt.

Sea makes fire!

Water flowing around the sea can change the weather. El Niño is a warm water current in the Pacific Ocean. Scientists think that this could cause droughts.

When is a lake not a lake?

When it's a mirage! A mirage often happens on a hot day. Hot air near the ground makes light from the bright sky bend upwards. This makes it seem as if there is a lake on the ground in the distance. Really the ground is dry!

People living in the desert

Drought

What happens when it doesn't rain?

Sometimes it is dry for a long time in places where it normally rains a lot. This is called a drought. There was a drought in the United States in the 1930s. Crops didn't grow and fields turned to dust. Many people had to leave their farms.

Does Earth have a blanket?

Planet Earth

Yes, it does. The Earth is wrapped in a thick blanket of air. It is called the atmosphere. This is where all the weather happens. The atmosphere also helps to keep the Earth's surface warm at night. In the day it protects us from harmful rays coming from the Sun.

Where does it rain every day?

In a tropical rainforest the weather is always very hot and very wet. The Sun shines every day, and there are downpours of heavy rain, too. Rainforest plants grow very quickly in this steamy weather.

Monsoon downpour!

In some countries it pours with rain for a few weeks every year. This is called a monsoon. In India, enough rain falls in one year to cover the ground with water 26 metres deep!

How deep is the atmosphere?

The atmosphere stretches hundreds of kilometres above our heads. If you go up through the atmosphere, the air gets thinner and thinner. High up in mountains, mountaineers find it difficult to breathe so they take breathing equipment with them.

Mountaineer

Look

Look at the picture of the Earth above. What do you think the white swirly patterns are?

Where does rain come from?

Most rain comes from the sea! Some seawater turns to gas in the air. If the air rises, the gas becomes water drops. These make clouds. If the drops get big enough, they fall as rain. The water flows back to the sea.

3. Rain falls

2. Water from plants rises into air

4. Water runs into rivers

1. Seawater rises into air

The water cycle

Head in the clouds!

The tops of tall mountains are often in the clouds. At the top it looks misty. Mountaineers sometimes get lost in these clouds!

Cirrus

Cumulus

Stratus

Are all clouds small and fluffy?

Clouds come in lots of different shapes and sizes. Weather experts give the different clouds names. Fluffy clouds are called cumulus clouds. Some are small and some are giant. Flat clouds are called stratus clouds. Wispy clouds high in the sky are called cirrus clouds.

What rain never lands?

Sometimes rain that falls from a cloud never reaches the ground. If the drops of rain fall into very dry air, the water in them turns into gas. This means that the drops disappear and never reach the ground.

Look

Look at the clouds outside today. Are they fluffy or flat? The picture above will help you.

What happens in a flood?

Sometimes a lot of rain falls in a few hours. So much water flows into rivers that they fill up and burst their banks. The rivers flood the land on each side. Sometimes houses disappear under the flood water.

Floods of tears!

The river Nile in Egypt floods every year. Thousands of years ago, the Egyptians made up a story about the flood. It said that a goddess called Isis cried so much that the river filled up with her tears.

Did Noah build an ark?

The Bible tells the story of a man called Noah. He built a great boat called an ark to escape a flood. We don't know if Noah's ark existed. Scientists have found out that there probably was a huge flood thousands of years ago.

Noah's ark

Flooded house

Find

Can you find the country of Egypt and the river Nile in an atlas?

Can there be a flood in a desert?

Yes there can. Most of the time there is no rain in a desert. The hot Sun bakes the ground hard. Once in a while, it rains heavily. The water flows off the ground instead of soaking in. This can cause a flood.

What is snow made of?

Snow is made of ice, which is water that has frozen. When it is very cold in a cloud, tiny bits of ice (crystals) begin to form, instead of water drops. The pieces clump together to make snowflakes that fall to the ground. The weather must be very cold for snow to fall. If it is too warm, the snowflakes melt and turn to rain.

Shiver!

Antarctica is the coldest place on Earth. The lowest temperature ever recorded there is −89°C. That's much, much colder than inside a freezer!

Snow drifts

Avalanche

When is snow dangerous?

When lots of snow falls on mountains, deep layers build up on the slopes. The snow may suddenly slide down the mountain. This is an avalanche. A big avalanche can bury a town. A loud noise or even a person walking on the snow can start an avalanche.

Are all snowflakes the same?

It's hard to believe, but all snowflakes are different – even though there are millions and millions of them. This is because every ice crystal in a snowflake has its own shape. No two crystals are the same. Most ice crystals in snowflakes looks like stars with six points.

Think

Can you think why it could be dangerous to ski across a steep hillside covered with snow?

Where are the fastest winds?

Inside a tornado. A tornado is like a spinning funnel made of air. They reach down from giant thunderstorms. The winds can blow at 480 kilometres an hour. That's twice as fast as an express train! Tornadoes can rip trees from the ground and destroy houses.

Tornado

Which storm has an eye?

A hurricane is a giant spinning storm made up of super-strong winds. The centre is a hole called the eye. Here it is calm and sunny. If a hurricane reaches land, the winds can damage buildings and heavy rain causes floods. Hurricane hunters are planes that fly into hurricanes to measure the wind speed.

Eye

Hurricane hunter

Stormy names!

A tropical storm that starts in the Atlantic Ocean is called a hurricane. In the Pacific Ocean, a tropical storm is called a typhoon. In the Indian Ocean it is called a cyclone.

Draw

Look at the pictures on this page. Can you draw a picture of a tornado and a hurricane?

How do we measure wind?

We measure the wind on a scale called the Beaufort Scale. The slowest wind is Force 1 on the scale. This is called a light breeze. The strongest wind is Force 12. This is called a hurricane. Force zero means there is no wind at all.

What makes the sky clap?

A thunderstorm! Inside a big thundercloud, water drops and bits of ice move up and down, bumping into each other. This makes electricity build up. When the electricity jumps around, we see a spark of lightning and hear a loud clap of thunder.

Huge hail!

Hail is made up of lumps of ice called hailstones. Hail can fall from thunderclouds. The biggest hailstone ever fell in Bangladesh in 1986. It was the size of a grapefruit!

When is lightning like a fork?

When lightning jumps from a thundercloud to the ground, it looks like huge forks in the sky. If lightning jumps from one cloud to another, the clouds light up. This is called sheet lightning. Lightning can be red, blue, yellow or white.

Lightning

Does lightning hit buildings?

Lightning often hits tall buildings. The buildings have a metal spike on top called a lightning conductor. When lightning hits a building, the lightning conductor carries the electricity to the ground. If there was no lightning conductor, the building could be damaged by the lightning.

Thundercloud

Count

Count the seconds between a flash of lightning and a clap of thunder. The bigger the number, the further away the thunderstorm.

What is a rainbow made of?

Rainbow

A rainbow is made of sunlight. The light bounces through raindrops. This splits the light into different colours. The colours of a rainbow are always the same. They are red, orange, yellow, green, blue, indigo and violet.

Remember

Can you remember all seven colours of a rainbow?

Northern lights

When does the sky have curtains?

In the far north and the far south of the world, amazing patterns of light sometimes appear in the sky. They look like colourful curtains. The patterns are called auroras (or-roar-rers). They happen when tiny light particles from the Sun smash into the air.

Rainbow with no colour!

A fogbow is a rainbow that is white. You might see a fogbow when the Sun shines through fog. It is white because the water drops in fog are too small to split up the light into rainbow colours.

When can you see three suns?

If there are thin clouds high in the sky, you might see three suns. The clouds are made of bits of ice. These bend light from the Sun. This makes it look as if there are two extra suns in the sky. We call these mock suns, or sun dogs.

What is a rain dance?

In many hot places, such as Africa, it only rains once or twice a year.

People may dance traditional rain dances if the rain does not fall. In the past, people believed that rain dances really could bring clouds and rain.

Who first recorded the weather?

Over 3000 years ago in China, people made notes about the weather. They studied how windy it was, or if it rained or snowed. They carved the information onto pieces of tortoiseshell.

Rain dance

Are weather sayings true?

There are many sayings about the weather. Most of them are true. One saying is 'Clear Moon, frost soon'. If there are no clouds in the sky you can see the Moon clearly. It also means it will get cold quickly at night. So the saying is true.

Full Moon

Weather cows!

Some people think that cows lie down when it is going to rain. But this weather saying is not true. Cows lie down on sunny days, too!

Discover

Can you find some more sayings about the weather? You could ask your teacher, or try looking in a book.

Which bird spins in the wind?

A metal cockerel on a weather vane. The cockerel spins so it can point in any direction. When the wind blows, the cockerel spins and points to where the wind is coming from. If the wind is blowing from the north, it is called a north wind. The wind blows from the north, south, east and west.

Weather vane

Groundhog Day!

In the USA, February 2 is called Groundhog Day. If people see an animal called a groundhog, they think that it will stay cold for another six weeks!

What is a weather house?

A weather house is a model that can tell how much moisture is in the air. If it is going to be dry, a lady in summer clothes comes out. If it is going to be rainy, a man with an umbrella comes out.

Weather house

How do we know how hot it is?

By reading a thermometer. A thermometer shows the temperature, which is how hot the air around us is. The first thermometer was made in 1714 by Gabriel Daniel Fahrenheit.

Think

From which direction does a southerly wind blow? North or south?

Can planes tell the weather?

Weather planes don't carry any passengers. Instead they fly through the air recording the weather. They measure the temperature of the air, the speed of the wind and how much water is in the air. This information helps weather forecasters tell us what the weather is going to be like.

Weather plane

Astronaut snaps!

Astronauts who travel on the space shuttle and live on space stations take cameras with them. They often take amazing photographs of clouds and thunderstorms from space.

Why do scientists fly balloons?

Scientists fly balloons to find out about the weather. The balloons are filled with a gas called helium. They float up through the air and carry instruments that measure the weather. The information is sent back to the ground by radio.

Weather balloon

Remember

Can you remember how information gets from a weather balloon down to the ground?

How do we watch weather from space?

With weather satellites. A satellite moves around the Earth in space. It takes photographs of the clouds below and sends them back to Earth. Satellite photographs show which way hurricanes are moving. They help forecasters to warn people if a hurricane is heading their way.

Did weather kill the dinosaurs?

Dinosaurs lived millions of years ago. Scientists think that they may have died because the weather all over the world got colder. They think this happened when a giant rock (meteorite) from space hit the Earth. This threw lots of dust into the air, which blocked out the Sun.

Meteorite hitting the Earth

Can trees affect the weather?

Yes, they can. Many rainforests are being cut down for farming. When trees are burned, the fires release a gas called carbon dioxide. This gas acts as a blanket over the Earth and does not let heat escape. High levels of carbon dioxide can raise the temperature too much causing damage to the Earth.

Rainforest

Windy tower!

The Tower of Winds is a tower in Athens, Greece. It was built 2000 years ago. It had a giant wind vane on top to measure the direction of the wind.

Find

Can you find Greenland on a map of the world?

Is our weather changing?

Weather experts think the weather is getting warmer. If the average world temperature rises by as little 1.5°C it will mean more storms, including hurricanes and tornadoes, and more droughts too.

Quiz time

Do you remember what you have read about weather? These questions will test your memory. The pictures will help you. If you get stuck, read the pages again.

1. Why do leaves fall in autumn?

page 101

2. When is a lake not a lake?

page 103

3. Where does it rain every day?

page 104

4. How deep is the atmosphere?

page 105

5. Are all clouds small and fluffy?

page 107

6. What rain never lands?

page 107

7. What happens in a flood?

page 108

11. What makes the sky clap?

page 114

8. Did Noah build an ark?

page 109

12. Who first recorded the weather?

page 118

13. What is a rain dance?

page 118

9. When is snow dangerous?

page 111

10. Which storm has an eye?

page 113

Answers

1. Because it is hard for them to grow in the dark winter months
2. When it's a mirage
3. In a tropical rainforest
4. Hundreds of kilometres
5. No, they come in different shapes and sizes
6. Drops that fall into very dry air
7. A lot of rain falls and floods the land
8. We don't know if Noah's ark existed
9. In an avalanche
10. A hurricane
11. A thunderstorm
12. The Chinese
13. A traditional dance to bring on clouds and rain

Questions about...

Is science in the playground?   130
What is a wheel?   131
What makes things stop and start? 131

Why do fireworks flash and bang? 132
Do I need energy?   133
What is a thermometer?   133

What is in an electric motor?   134
Where do rainbow colours
    come from?   135
What is the loudest sound?   135

Where is science in a city?   136
Who works railway signals?   137
How do skyscrapers stay up?   137

How do you make magnets?   138
Does a magnet have a field?   139
What are poles?   139

Where does electricity come from? 140
What is a circuit?   141
When is electricity in the sky?   141

What waves are invisible?   142
What is an X-ray?   143
What waves can cook food?   143

Are computers clever?   144
Does a computer have a brain?   145
How does a computer remember? 145

Science

What do scientists do at work? 150
Who is the most famous scientist? 151
Do scientists help doctors? 151

Are animals part of science? 152
What is an ecologist? 153
How do ecologists follow animals? 153

Is the Internet like a web? 146
What does www stand for? 146
Can I use the Internet without
   a computer? 147

Can a car be made from card? 148
What materials grow? 149
Does glass grow? 149

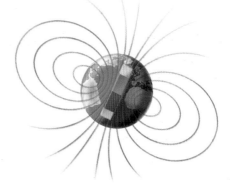

Are we harming the Earth? 154
What is recycling? 155
Does electricity harm the Earth? 155

Quiz time 156

Is science in the playground?

Yes, it is! Lots of science happens in a playground. The playground rides could not work without science. A see-saw is a simple machine called a lever. It has a long arm and a point in the middle called a pivot. As you ride on the see-saw, the lever tips up and down on the pivot.

See-saw

Lever

Pivot

Sloping machine!

A ramp is the simplest machine of all. It is easier to walk up a ramp to the top of a hill than it is to climb a steep hillside.

What is a wheel?

A wheel is a very simple machine that can spin around. Wheels let other machines, such as skateboards, bicycles, cars and trains, roll along smoothly. They also make it easy to move heavy weights in carts and wheelbarrows.

Feel

Press the palm of your hand onto a table. A force called friction stops you sliding your hand along.

What makes things stop and start?

Pushes and pulls make things stop and start. Scientists use the word 'force' for pushes and pulls. Forces are all around us. The force of gravity pulls things downwards. It makes a rollercoaster car hurtle downhill. It also slows the car on the uphill parts of the track.

Rollercoaster

Why do fireworks flash and bang?

Fireworks flash and bang because they are full of chemicals that burn. The chemicals have lots of energy stored in them. When they burn, the energy changes to light, heat and sound. We use chemicals that burn in other places too, such as cookers, heaters and car engines.

Fireworks

How do candles burn?

Candles are made of wax and a wick (string). When the wick is lit, the wax around it melts. The wick then soaks up the liquid wax and the heat of the flame turns the wax into a gas (vapour), which burns away. As the wax becomes vapour it cools the wick, allowing the candle to burn slowly.

Hot! Hot! Hot!

The hottest-ever temperature recorded was in a science laboratory. It was four hundred million degrees Celsius (400,000,000°C).

What is a thermometer?

A thermometer tells us how hot something is. This is called temperature. The numbers written on a thermometer are normally degrees Celsius (°C). If you put a thermometer in cold water, it shows 0°C. If you put it in boiling water it shows 100°C. A thermometer can also measure your body temperature.

Remember

Which piece of equipment is used to measure how hot or cold something is?

What is in an electric motor?

Magnets and wires. Electricity from a battery passes through the wires. This turns the wires into a magnet. Two more magnets on each side of the motor push and pull against the wires. This makes a thin metal rod (spindle) spin around.

Battery

Wires

White light

Prism (glass triangle)

Electricity flows along wires

Magnet on side of motor

Spindle

Why does light bend?

Light rays travel in straight lines. When light shines through a prism, the rays bend because light travels more slowly through glass than air. Sunlight is called white light, but it is made up of a mixture of colours. When white light passes through a prism it splits into many colours, like a rainbow.

Fast as light!

Light is the fastest thing in the Universe. It travels 300,000 kilometres every second. That means it could travel around the Earth seven times in less than a second!

Rainbow colours

Make

On a sunny day, stand with your back to the Sun. Spray water into the air and you should see a rainbow!

What is the loudest sound?

The roar of a jet engine is the loudest sound we normally hear. It is thousands of times louder than someone shouting. Sounds this loud can damage our ears if we are too close to them. The quietest sounds we can hear are things like rustling leaves.

Where is science in a city?

Everywhere! In a big city, almost every machine, building and vehicle is based on science. Cars, buses and trains help us move around the city. Scientists and engineers have also worked out how to build tall skyscrapers where people live and work.

City

Look

Look at the city picture. How many different forms of transport can you see?

Railway signals

Who works railway signals?

Nobody does! The signals work by themselves. Electronic parts on the track work out if a train is passing. Then a computer changes the signals to red, to stop another train moving onto the same piece of track.

How do skyscrapers stay up?

Skyscrapers stay up because they have a strong frame on the inside. The frame is made from steel and concrete. These are very strong materials. Normally you can't see the frame. It is hidden by the skyscraper's walls. The walls hang on the frame.

Plane spotters!

There's science at an airport, too. A radar machine uses radio waves to find aircraft in the sky. This helps people at the airport to guide the aircraft onto the runway.

How do you make magnets?

By using another magnet! Magnets are made from lumps of iron or steel. You can turn a piece of iron into a magnet by stroking it with another magnet. A magnet can also be made by sending electricity through a coil of wire. This is called an electromagnet. Some electromagnets are so strong, they can pick up cars.

Electromagnet picking up scrap cars

Count

Find a magnet at home (you can use a fridge magnet). How many paper clips can your magnet pick up?

Does a magnet have a field?

Yes – but it's not a field of grass! The area around a magnet is called a magnetic field. A magnetic field is shown by drawing lines around a magnet. The Earth has a magnetic field, too. It is as though there is a giant magnet inside the Earth.

Magnetic field around the Earth

What are poles?

Every magnet has two poles. These are where the pull of a magnet is strongest. They are called the north pole and the south pole. A north pole and a south pole always pull towards each other. Two north poles always push each other away. So do two south poles.

Handy rock!

Some rocks act like magnets. Years ago, people used magnetic rocks to find their way. If they let the rock spin round, it always pointed in the same direction.

Where does electricity come from?

Battery →

Electricity comes to your home along cables from power stations. The cables are held off the ground by pylons. Around your home are holes in the wall called sockets. When a machine is plugged into a socket, electricity flows out to work the machine.

Electric!

Our homes are full of machines that work using electricity. If there was no electricity we wouldn't have televisions, lights, washing machines or computers!

Power station

Remember

Mains electricity is very dangerous. It could kill you. Never play with mains sockets in your home.

Light bulb

Switch

Pylon holds
cables
off the
ground

What is a circuit?

A circuit is a loop that electricity moves around. This circuit is made up of a battery, a light bulb and a switch. If the switch is turned on, the loop would be broken. Then the electricity would stop moving and the light would go out.

When is electricity in the sky?

When there's a thunderstorm! During a storm, a kind of electricity called static electricity builds up. This can make a big flash, that lights up the sky. This is lightning. The hot lightning heats up the air around it and this makes a loud clap. This is thunder.

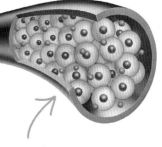

Electricity flows
along the cables

What waves are invisible?

Radio waves are all around us, but we can't see them. We use radio waves to send sounds and pictures to radios and televisions. Some radio waves come from satellites in space. A radio set receives radio waves through a metal rod called an aerial. A dish-shaped aerial picks up radio waves for television programmes.

Satellite

Radio waves

Aerial

Remember
Which part of your body would stop an X-ray? Skin or bone?

Radio

X-ray machine

Picture of bone

Dish-shaped aerial

What is an X-ray?

An X-ray is like a radio wave. X-rays can go through the soft bits of your body. However, hard bones stop them. That's why doctors use X-ray machines to take pictures of the inside of people's bodies.

Space radio!

Radio waves can travel through space. But they can't travel through water. So you can listen to a radio in a space station, but not in a submarine!

What waves can cook food?

Microwaves can. These are a kind of radio wave. They have lots of energy in them. A microwave uses this energy to cook food. Microwaves are fired into the oven. They make the particles in the food jiggle about. This makes the food hot.

Are computers clever?

Not really! Computers are amazing machines, but they can only do what they are told. They carry out computer programs written down by people. These are full of instructions that the computer follows. You can also tell a computer what to do by using its keyboard and mouse.

Remember

Can you remember the name for a computer's electronic brain? Read these pages again to help you.

Keyboard

Microchip

Close-up of microchip

Does a computer have a brain?

A computer doesn't have a brain like yours. It has an electronic brain called a central processing unit. This is a microchip the size of your fingernail. This amazing mini machine can do millions of difficult sums in a split second.

Screen

How does a computer remember?

A computer remembers with its electronic memory. This is made up of lots of tiny microchips. When you turn the computer off, everything in the memory is lost. So you have to save your work on a disc, otherwise you lose it when you switch off.

Mouse

Computer room!

The first computer was made 60 years ago. It was so big that it filled a whole room. A modern calculator can do sums much more quickly!

Is the Internet like a web?

The Internet is made up of millions of computers around the world. They are connected like a giant spider's web! A computer connects to a machine called a modem. This sends signals to a server. The server lets you connect to the Internet. People can send emails and open web pages.

Email

Find out

Look at the main picture on these pages. See if you can find out what the word 'email' is short for.

What does www stand for?

The letters www are short for World Wide Web. The World Wide Web is like a giant library of information, stored on computers all over the world. There are also thousands of shops on the World Wide Web, where you can buy almost anything.

Can I use the Internet without a computer?

Yes. Other machines can link to the Internet, too. You can see simple information from the Internet on a mobile phone. You can send and get emails, too. A mobile phone connects to the Internet by radio.

Mobile phone

Web page

Millions of pages!

The World Wide Web has more than 8000 million pages of information. That's two pages for every person on the planet!

Can a car be made from card?

Yes, it can – but it would break if you sat inside it! It is always important to use the right material to make something. Cars are made from tough, long-lasting materials. Metal, plastic and rubber are all materials used to make cars.

A racing car is made up of hundreds of parts and different materials

Think

Think of three more materials from which things are made. If you get stuck, ask an adult.

Cotton plants make clothes

What materials grow?

Many of the materials we use every day come from plants. Wood comes from the trunks and branches of trees. Cotton is made from the seeds of cotton plants to make clothes such as T-shirts. Some rubber is made from a liquid (sap) from rubber trees.

Rubber tree makes tyres

Tree trunks and branches make wooden bats

Does glass grow?

Glass doesn't grow! It is made from sand and two other materials called limestone and soda. These materials are mixed together and melted to make a gooey liquid. When the mixture cools down, it forms the hard glass that we use to makes windows, drinking glasses and other objects.

Bullet proof!

Some glass is extra-strong. Toughened glass is so hard that even a bullet from a gun bounces off it!

What do scientists do at work?

Some scientists try to find out about the world around us. Others find out about space, planets and stars. Some scientists discover useful materials that we can use. Scientists carry out experiments in laboratories to test their ideas.

Scientist in a laboratory

Who is the most famous scientist?

The most famous scientist is called Albert Einstein (1879–1955). He made many discoveries about time, space, the force of gravity and nuclear energy. The ideas that Einstein wrote down were so amazing that they made him famous across the world.

$$=mc^2$$

Albert Einstein

Atom pie!

One hundred years ago, scientists thought that the pieces in an atom were all spread out, like the raisins in a pudding. Now we know they are all bunched together.

Do scientists help doctors?

Yes, they do. Many scientists make medicines that the doctor gives you when you are ill. They also help to make the complicated machines that doctors use in hospitals. Scientists also try to find out what makes us ill, and how we can stay healthy.

Find

Find out the name of the country where Albert Einstein was born. An encyclopedia will help you.

Are animals part of science?

Yes, they are! Scientists who study animals and plants work everywhere in the world. They study in hot rainforests, dusty deserts, high mountains, at the freezing poles and in rivers and seas.

Many scientists study animals and plants

Look

Study the picture. Can you see something that might harm the animals and plants?

Which way?

Some animals travel great distances around the world. They use the Earth's magnetic field to guide them.

What is an ecologist?

An ecologist is a scientist. Ecologists study where plants and animals live. They also look at how plants and animals live alongside each other, and the things that animals eat. Ecologists study the harm that we do to plants and animals.

How do ecologists follow animals?

With complicated radio equipment. First they catch the animal and put a collar on its neck, wing or leg. The collar has a tiny radio aerial that sends out radio waves. The ecologist finds the animal by listening with a machine that picks up the radio waves.

Are we harming the Earth?

Many of the things we do are harming the world around us. Machines such as cars put dangerous gases into the air. These gases can harm plants and make people ill. They are also making the weather change. Scientists are always looking for new ways to reduce damage to the Earth.

Pollution

Dirty cars!

Cars and other vehicles can produce so much pollution that in some cities it has become difficult for people to breathe.

What is recycling?

Recycling is using materials again, instead of throwing them away. This helps to make less waste. Ask your parents to take empty glass bottles to a bottle bank. The glass in the bottles is made into new bottles. Paper, metal and plastic are also recycled.

1. Bottle bank

2. Bottles are crushed

3. Glass is melted

4. Liquid glass is put in moulds

5. New bottles are ready

Glass recycling

Save

Ask your family to save electricity. Get them to switch off the lights when nobody is in the room.

Does electricity harm the Earth?

Yes, it does. Lots of coal, oil and gas are burned to make electricity. These make harmful gases that go into the air. You can help by turning things off to save electricity. Scientists are inventing new ways of making electricity from the wind, the Sun and water.

Quiz time

Do you remember what you have read about science? These questions will test your memory. The pictures will help you. If you get stuck, read the pages again.

1. Is science in the playground?

page 130

2. How do candles burn?

page 133

3. What is a thermometer?

page 133

4. What is in an electric motor?

page 134

5. How do skyscrapers stay up?

page 137

6. Does a magnet have a field?

page 139

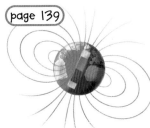

7. What is a circuit?

page 141

page 146

11. What does www stand for?

8. What is an X-ray?

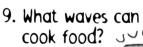

page 143

12. Who is the most famous scientist?

$E=mc^2$

page 151

9. What waves can cook food?

page 143

13. Does electricity harm the Earth?

page 155

page 144

10. Are computers clever?

Answers

1. Yes it is, in rides such as see-saws
2. By melting wax, which becomes a vapour that burns.
3. A machine that measures heat
4. Magnets and wires
5. They have a strong frame that supports them
6. Yes, a magnetic field
7. When the candle is lit, the wax melts and disappears into the air
8. It is a radio wave
9. Microwaves
10. No, but they can follow instructions
11. World Wide Web
12. Albert Einstein
13. Yes, it can

Questions about...

What were the first inventions?   160
How did early people see
  in the dark?   160
Who invented the wheel?   161

Who invented the first car?   162
Why do tractors have such
  big tyres?   163
What was a boneshaker?   163

Who used the
  first sails?   164
Why did coal
  miners need
  steam power?   165
Can trains float?   165

What is a combine harvester?   166
Can ships fly?   167
Did people pull ploughs?   167

Who invented jumbo jets?   168
Can balloons carry people?   169
Do planes perform tricks?   169

How can we see into space?   170
Who invented spectacles?   171
How can we make small
  things bigger?   171

Who made the streets light up?   172
How big was the first computer?   173
Who made electricity from
  the wind?   173

Inventions

Why do clocks have hands? 174
How does the Sun tell the time? 175
Can candles tell the time? 175

When was cooking invented? 176
Who wrote the first words? 177
Who made the first phone call? 177

What is special about the shuttle? 182
Who invented fireworks? 183
Can people live in space? 183

Do zips have teeth? 184
How did teddy bears get
   their name? 185
Which horse can rock? 185

What was a gramophone? 178
Who invented television? 179
Who took the first photo? 179

Why were fridges dangerous? 180
How do microwaves cook food? 181
Have toilets always flushed? 181

Quiz time 186

What were the first inventions?

The first inventions were stone tools, which early people began to make about two million years ago. During the Stone Age, about 30,000 years ago, people discovered how to sew animal skins together to make clothes. They also learnt how to keep warm and dry by building shelters.

Stone Age people using tools ↗

How did early people see in the dark?

Prehistoric people used lamps to light up caves. The lamps were made of clay or stone saucers, which were filled with animal fat. The animal fat was then burnt using a wick made of moss.

Fire-makers!

Early people discovered how to make fire more than 250,000 years ago! Thousands of years later, flint stones were used to make sparks, which lit dried grass and wood.

Who invented the wheel?

The Sumerian people invented wheels 5500 years ago. They were heavy and made with carved wood that was fastened together. Later, the ancient Egyptians made spoked wheels, which were lighter.

Count

In this book, how many inventions can you find that use the wheel?

Spoked wheels

Who invented the first car?

Karl Benz invented the first car in 1896. It had a petrol-powered engine but could not travel very fast. The first popular car was the Model T, built in 1908 by the Ford company in the United States. Over 15 million of them were sold worldwide.

Model T Ford

Why do tractors have such big tyres?

Tractors were invented in 1892 and are used to pull farm machinery, such as ploughs. Tractors have huge tyres to stop them getting stuck in mud. Big weights at the front stop tractors tipping over when pulling heavy machinery.

Tractor

Wooden lines!

Railway tracks were once made of wood! Wheels move more easily along rails, so horses pulled wagons on wooden rails more than 400 years ago. Metal rails were invented in 1789.

What was a boneshaker?

A boneshaker was one of the first bicycles. It had solid tyres and was so uncomfortable to ride that it made people's bones shake. In 1888, John Dunlop invented air-filled rubber tyres that made cycling more comfortable.

Try

If you have a bike, try riding it in the garden. Is it a smooth or bumpy ride?

Who used the first sails?

Sails were invented by the Egyptians more than 5000 years ago. About 2000 years ago, the best sailors were the Phoenician people. They sailed in boats made of cedar wood and reeds. These ships had sails and oars and were used to make long journeys.

Draw

Using coloured pens or pencils, draw your own super sail boat. Try adding your own amazing inventions.

Phoenician boat

Super sailing!
Modern boats use inventions such as machines that roll up the sails and special gears that let the boat steer itself.

Why did coal miners need steam power?

Before steam power, miners had to pull coal carts out of mines by hand. This was very hard work. Then in 1814, a coal miner named George Stephenson invented an engine that pulled the carts out of the mines using steam power.

Maglev train

Can trains float?

Yes they can, in a way. In 1909 Robert Goddard discovered a way to make trains travel using magnets. These trains are called Maglevs. They run on a magnetic rail that pushes the train up so it seems to be floating. Maglevs can reach very high speeds.

What is a combine harvester?

A combine harvester is a big farm machine that cuts crops and separates grain. The first combine harvester was invented in 1836 and was pulled by horses. Today, farmers all over the world use these machines so they can harvest their crops quickly.

Combine harvester

Plant power!

Scientists are changing the way plants grow. They have invented ways of creating crops with built-in protection from pests and diseases.

Can ships fly?

Airships can! They are filled with a special gas called helium. This gas is lighter than air, and makes the airship float in the sky. Today, airships are used to display adverts in the sky and are not used for people to travel in.

Airship

Did people pull ploughs?

Ploughs were invented in Egypt around 2000 BC and were first pulled by people. They helped farmers break up the ground and turn the soil over. Later, people began to use horses and oxen to pull ploughs.

Think

Can you think of any other machines or animals that you would find on a farm?

167

Who invented jumbo jets?

A jumbo jet is a plane. In 1970, the first jumbo jet flight took place between New York and London. The planes are powered by jet engines that were invented by Dr Hans von Ohain of Germany, and Sir Frank Whittle of England. Their inventions developed to become modern jet engines.

Jumbo jet

Bird brains!

Many inventors have tried to fly by flapping birdlike wings. All have failed. One of the first bird-men crashed to his death at a Roman festival in the 1st century AD.

Can balloons carry people?

Hot-air balloons were invented in 1783. They can carry people high up into the sky. The first ever passengers to fly in a hot air balloon were not humans but a cockeral, a duck and a sheep!

Do planes perform tricks?

Yes, they do. The Red Arrows are a team of highly skilled pilots that can make their planes perform tricks. Their red aircrafts can fly upside down and on their sides and are very fast. The Red Arrows perform in front of large crowds at airshows and other special occasions.

Make

With some paper, make a plane and colour it in. How far can you get it to fly?

The Red Arrows

How can we see into space?

People can look at the stars and planets by using a telescope. The first telescope was invented by a Dutchman called Hans Lippershey in 1608. In 1609, the Italian scientist Galileo built his own telescope. He was the first person to see the craters on the Moon.

Telescope

Who invented spectacles?

The Italians did. In the 14th century in Italy people made their own glass lenses to look through. These small lenses were put into frames and were used to help people to read.

Write

Imagine you have found a pair of magic spectacles. Write a story about what you see when you put them on.

How can we make small things bigger?

By using a microscope. A microscope uses pieces of glass called lenses. These make small things look bigger than they really are. The first microscope was invented in the 1600s and had one lens. Later microscopes had two lenses to make them more powerful.

Microscope

Marvellous maths!

Around AD 300, the Chinese invented a counting machine called an abacus. It was a wooden frame with beads strung on wires and it helped people do complicated sums.

Who made the streets light up?

Street lamp

An Austrian named Carl Auer did, in the late 1800s. He invented a lamp called a gas mantle that glowed very brightly when heated up. The gas mantle was used in the first street lamps. Long torches were needed to light the lamps.

Wind power!

The first windmills were invented thousands of years ago. They helped to grind grain into flour. Today, windmills are used to pump water, make electricity and power machinery.

How big was the first computer?

The first computer was so big that it took up a whole room. In 1975, the first home computers were made but they were expensive and not very powerful. Computers today are small, cheap and powerful.

Wind turbine

Who made electricity from the wind?

In 1888, Charles F Brush invented a modern-day windmill called a wind turbine. Wind turbines have blades that turn in the wind. These power a motor inside the turbine, which makes electricity. Wind turbines can power entire towns.

Remember

In ancient times, what was the name of the counting machine that was invented by the Chinese?

Why do clocks have hands?

Clocks have hands so that people can tell the time. The hands point to different numbers on the clock face and these tell us what time it is. Clocks work by using a series of springs and wheels that move the hands of the clock around. The first mechanical alarm clock was invented in 1787.

Make

Use a paper plate to make a clock. Write the numbers on the face and use plastic straws for the hands.

Alarm clock

174

How does the Sun tell the time?

The Sun was used to help people tell the time before clocks were invented. Sundials have a stone face marked with the hours, and a pointer that makes a shadow when the Sun is shining on it. Whatever hour the shadow falls on is the time at that moment.

Sun dial

Watch it!

The wrist watch was invented in the 1600s by a French mathematician. He attached a piece of string to his pocket watch and tied it around his wrist.

Can candles tell the time?

Candles were once used as clocks to tell the time. They were marked with rings so that when the wax burnt down, people could tell how much time has passed by.

When was cooking invented?

Cooking was invented in prehistoric times by some of our earliest relatives. When people discovered fire, they realized that if food was placed in the fire, it tasted better. Cooking also made food safer because it killed germs that might cause sickness.

The first cooks

Who wrote the first words?

The Sumerian people wrote the first words more than 5500 years ago. They scratched words onto clay tablets. The first writing was made up of pictures. Ancient picture-writing used hundreds of different signs. Today, modern alphabets have far fewer letters.

Write

Using pictures instead of words, write a secret message. Can your friends work out what it says?

Alexander Graham Bell

Smoky signals!

Before inventions such as the telephone, sending long-distance messages had to be simple. Native Americans used smoke signals to send messages to each other.

Who made the first phone call?

Alexander Graham Bell made the first telephone call in 1876. The telephone worked by turning vibrations in the human voice into electrical signals. These signals travelled down a wire to another phone, where they were turned back into sound.

What was a gramophone?

In 1887, Emile Berlin invented a machine that could play music. The machine was called a gramophone. To make it work, a handle was turned, which turned a disc under a steel needle. The needle allowed the music to play.

Gramophone

Find out

Today we use CDs to play music. Can you find out what the letters CD are short for?

Marvellous movies!

Only one person at a time could watch the very first films. The viewer went into a special room and looked through a hole in a box.

Who invented television?

John Logie Baird invented the first television in 1926. The pictures were black and white and very blurry. Modern televisions show clear, sharp pictures in colour.

Flat screen television

Who took the first photo?

Joseph Nicephore took the first-ever photograph in 1826. The picture was of rooftops and took eight hours to take. The first cameras were very big, and instead of paper, the photos were printed on glass plates.

Why were fridges dangerous?

The first electric refrigerators were invented in 1805, but they were dangerous to use. This was because they used a poisonous gas to keep them cold. In 1929, a safer gas called freon was used. However freon causes damage to the planet, so scientists want to change this, too.

Stone cold!

Stone Age people invented the first refrigerators! They buried any spare food in pits dug in ground that was always frozen.

Early fridge

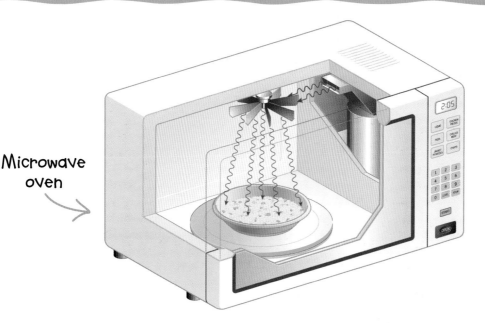

Microwave oven

How do microwaves cook food?

A microwave oven produces waves that make food heat itself up. In 1945, Percy L. Spencer invented the microwave oven after noticing that a microwave machine at his workplace had melted a chocolate bar in his pocket.

Look

Take a look around your house. How many inventions help you and your family every day?

Have toilets always flushed?

4000 years ago in Greece, royal palaces had flushing toilets that used rainwater. Thomas Twyford invented the first ceramic flushing toilet in 1885. His design is still used today.

What is special about the shuttle?

The space shuttle is a very special spacecraft. This is because it is reusable. Most spacecraft can only go into space once, but the shuttle is like a space plane. It can return into space up to ten times. The first space shuttle was launched in 1981.

Space shuttle →

Who invented fireworks?

The Chinese invented fireworks thousands of years ago. The loud sound that they made was supposed to frighten off evil spirits. Today, fireworks are used to celebrate special occasions.

Write

Imagine you are living on board a space station. Write a letter to tell people about your adventure.

Fast flyer!

Concorde was a superfast plane that flew people across the Atlantic in record time. Trips from London to New York only took three hours.

Space station

Can people live in space?

Yes, they can. A space station is a home in space for astronauts. It has a kitchen for making meals, and cabins with sleeping bags. The first space station was launched in 1971.

Do zips have teeth?

Yes, zips do have teeth! A zip has two rows of teeth that can be opened and shut by a slider. The first zip was invented in 1891. It was called the Talon Slide Fastener and was used on a boot called the zipper. This is where the zip got its name from.

Zip ⟶

Bone brush!

The first toothbrush was made out of animal bone. The bone had small holes drilled into it where bristles were placed.

How did teddy bears get their name?

The teddy bear was named after US President Theodore Roosevelt in 1903. The president's nickname was Teddy. One day he spared the life of a bear cub when out hunting. The teddy bear became the most popular soft toy ever.

Which horse can rock?

The rocking horse was invented in 1780. It was a toy horse that children could ride on without hurting themselves. Early rocking horses were usually dapple-grey in colour and rocked on wooden bow rockers.

Draw

Design your own perfect toy. Draw a picture of it and colour it in.

Rocking horse

185

Quiz time

Do you remember what you have read about inventions? These questions will test your memory. The pictures will help you. If you get stuck, read the pages again.

page 160

1. How did early people see in the dark?

page 161

2. Who invented the wheel?

3. What was a boneshaker?

page 163

4. Can trains float?

page 165

5. Did people pull ploughs?

page 167

6. Can ships fly?

page 167

7. Who invented jumbo jets?

11. Who took the first photo?

page 182

8. Who invented spectacles?

page 171

12. What is special about the shuttle?

page 183

9. How does the Sun tell the time?

page 175

13. Who invented fireworks?

10. Who wrote the first words?

page 177

Answers

1. They used lamps made of clay and animal fat
2. The Sumerian people
3. One of the very first bicycles
4. Yes, the Maglev train can
5. Yes, the first ploughs were pulled by people
6. Airships can fly
7. Dr Hans von Ohain
8. The Italians
9. With a sundial
10. The Sumerian people
11. Joseph Niocephore
12. It can be reused
13. The Chinese

187

Questions about...

Why do babies grip so tightly? 190
When do babies start to walk? 191
Am I always learning? 191

What does my skin do? 192
How thick is my skin? 193
Why do I sweat when I'm warm? 193

How much hair do
    I have? 194
What are nails
    made from? 195
Why do we
    have fingernails? 195

How many bones do I have? 196
What are bones made from? 197
How are bones joined together? 197

How do muscles work? 198
What is my biggest muscle? 198
What makes my muscles move? 199

Why do I need to breathe? 200
Is my voice kept in a box? 201
What makes air go into
    my lungs? 201

What food is good for me? 202
Why do I need to eat food? 203
What happens when I swallow? 203

Your Body

What are teeth made of? 204

How many sets of teeth do
I have? 204

What happens to the food
I swallow? 205

Why does my heart beat? 206
What does blood do? 207
Does blood get dirty? 207

Why can't I see smells? 210
How do I taste things? 211
How many smells can I sense? 211

Is my brain really big? 212
Can my brain really wave? 213
How does my brain help
me to play? 213

Are my eyes like a camera? 208
What is inside my ears? 209
How do I hear sounds? 209

How can I stay healthy? 214
What can make me sick? 215
Why do I have injections? 215

Quiz time 216

Why do babies grip so tightly?

Tiny babies can do simple things. If something touches a baby's cheek, it turns its head and tries to suck. If something touches the baby's hand, it grips tightly. These actions are called reflexes. They help the baby survive.

Giant baby!

A baby grows quickly before it is born. If it grew this fast for 50 years, it would be taller than Mount Everest!

Baby gripping

When do babies start to walk?

When they are about one year old. Babies can roll over at three months. At six months, they can sit up. At nine months they start to crawl. Then babies learn to stand and take their first steps.

Children playing

Am I always learning?

Yes, you are! Most children start school when they are five years old. They learn to count, read, write and draw. Children learn outside of the classroom, too. Playing and having fun with friends is a great way to learn new things!

Find out

Find out three reasons why a newborn baby cries? Ask a grown-up if you need any help.

What does my skin do?

Skin protects you from bumps and scratches. It stops your body from drying out, and prevents germs from getting in. When you play on bikes or skateboards, you should wear gloves and knee pads to protect your skin.

Knee pads protect from cuts

Gloves protect from scrapes

Ouch! Ouch! Ouch!

There are millions of tiny touch sensors in your skin. They tell your brain when something touches your skin. Some sensors feel hot and cold. Others feel pain. Ouch!

Hair

Layers of the skin

Epidermis

Dermis

Touch sensor

How thick is my skin?

Your skin is very thin. It is only 2 millimetres thick. On top is a layer of tough, dead cells called the epidermis. These cells gradually rub off. New cells grow underneath to replace them. Underneath is another layer of skin called the dermis. This contains areas that give you your sense of touch.

Think

If you are riding a bike or playing on a skateboard, what should you wear on your head, and why?

Why do I sweat when I'm warm?

To cool down again. Your body warms up on a hot day or when you run about. You sweat to get rid of the heat. Your body lets sweat out through your skin. As the sweat dries, it takes away heat. This cools you down.

How much hair do I have?

 Your whole body is covered in about five million hairs! You have about 100,000 hairs on your head. Hair grows out of tiny pits in your skin, called follicles. Hair grows in different colours and it can be wavy, curly or straight.

Blonde wavy hair

Red straight hair

Black straight hair

Black curly hair

For the chop!

The hair on your head grows about 2 millimetres a week. If a hair is never cut, it reaches about one metre in length before it falls out. It is replaced by a new hair.

What are nails made from?

Fingernails and toenails are made from a hard material called keratin. It is the same material that hair is made from. Nails grow out of the nail root. In a week, a nail grows by about half a millimetre. They grow faster at night than in the day!

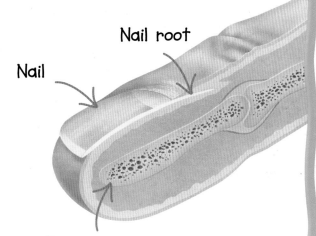

Nail root

Nail

Finger bone

Look

Have a look in the mirror. Is your hair straight, wavy or curly? Use the pictures on page 194 to help you.

Why do we have fingernails?

Fingernails protect your fingertips. The nail stops your fingertip bending back when you touch something. This helps your fingers to feel things. Nails are useful for picking up tiny objects.

How many bones do I have?

Most people have 206 bones. Half of them are in your hands and feet. All your bones together make up your skeleton. The skeleton is like a frame. It holds up the other parts of your body. It also protects the squashy bits inside.

Find

Can you find your collarbone? It starts at your shoulder and runs to the top of your rib cage.

Skeleton key

1. Skull
2. Collar bone
3. Shoulder blade
4. Ribs
5. Upper arm bone
6. Pelvis
7. Thigh bone
8. Kneecap
9. Calf bone
10. Shin bone

What are bones made from?

Bones are made from different materials mixed together. Some of the materials are very hard and some are tough and bendy. Together they make bones very strong. There is a kind of jelly called marrow inside some bones. This makes tiny parts for your blood, called red and white cells.

Marrow

Spongy bone

Hard bone

Strong bones!

Your bone is lightweight but super-strong. It is stronger than concrete or steel, which are used for making buildings and bridges! But bones can still break if they are bent too much.

How are bones joined together?

Your bones are connected by joints. They let your back, arms, legs, fingers and toes move. You have about 100 joints. The largest joints are in your hips and knees. The smallest joints are inside your ear.

How do muscles work?

Muscles are made from fibres that look like bits of string. The fibres get shorter to make the muscle pull. Many muscles make your bones move. They help you to run, jump, hold and lift things. Some muscles move your eyes, your heart and other body parts.

Muscle fibre

Nerve

What is my biggest muscle?

The biggest muscles in your body are the ones that you sit on – your bottom! You use them when you walk and run. The strongest muscle in your body is in your jaw. It scrunches your teeth together.

Muscle

What makes my muscles move?

Your brain does. It sends messages along nerves to your muscles. Lots of muscles are needed, even for small movements, like writing with a pen. Your brain controls other muscles without you thinking about it. For example, the muscles in your heart keep working even when you are asleep.

Why do I need to breathe?

You breathe to take air into your body. There is a gas in the air called oxygen that your body needs to work.

The air goes up your nose or into your mouth. Then it goes down a tube called the windpipe and into your lungs.

1. Air goes into your nose or mouth

2. Air goes down the windpipe

3. Air enters the lungs

Count
How many times do you breathe in and out in one minute?

Is my voice kept in a box?

Not quite! The real name for your voicebox is the larynx. It's at the top of the windpipe, and makes a bulge at the front of your neck. Air passing through the voicebox makes it shake, or vibrate. This is the sound of your voice. Your voice can make lots of sounds, and helps you to sing!

Singing

What makes air go into my lungs?

There is a big muscle under your lungs that moves down. More muscles make your ribs move out. This makes your lungs bigger. Air rushes into your lungs to fill the space. When your muscles relax, the air is pushed out again.

Fill 'em up!

When you are resting, you take in enough air to fill a can of fizzy drink in every breath. When you are running, you breathe in ten times as much air.

What food is good for me?

Lots of food is good for you! Different foods give your body the goodness it needs. Fruit and vegetables are very good for you. Bread and pasta give you energy. Small amounts of fat, such as cheese, keep your nerves healthy. Chicken and fish keep your muscles strong.

Fats keep nerves healthy

Vegetables help digestion

Fruit is full of goodness

Eating elephants!

You eat about one kilogram of food every day. During your life, you will eat about 30 tonnes of food. That's the same weight as six elephants!

Bread gives energy

Fish helps muscles to grow strong

Why do I need to eat food?

Food keeps your body working. It is like fuel for your body. It keeps your body going through the day and night, and works your muscles. Food also contains things your body needs to grow, repair itself and fight illness.

Your whole body needs food

What happens when I swallow?

The first thing you do with food is chew it. Then you swallow lumps of the chewed food. When you swallow, the food goes down a tube called the gullet. Muscles in the gullet push the food down into your stomach.

Draw

Look at some of the pictures on these pages. Can you draw a healthy meal that you would like to eat?

What are teeth made of?

Teeth are covered in a material called enamel. This is harder than most kinds of rock! Teeth are fixed into your jaw bones by roots. Sharp front teeth (incisors) bite food into small pieces. Tall, pointy teeth (canines) tear and pull food. Flat back teeth (molars) chew food to a mush.

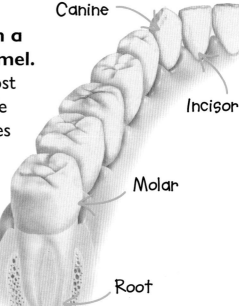

Canine

Incisor

Molar

Root

How many sets of teeth do I have?

You have two sets. A baby is born without teeth. The first set of teeth appears when a child is six months old. This set has 20 teeth. These teeth fall out at about seven years old. They are replaced by 32 adult teeth.

Discover
Do you still have your first set of teeth, or have your baby teeth begun to fall out?

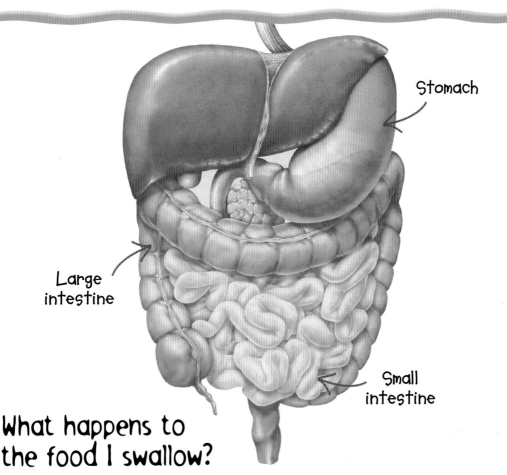

Stomach

Large intestine

Small intestine

What happens to the food I swallow?

The food you swallow goes into your stomach. Here, special juices and strong muscles break the food up into a thick mush. The mushy food then goes into a long tube called the intestines. Here, all the goodness from the food is taken out, to be used by our body.

All gone!

When you go to the toilet, you get rid of waste. This is leftover food. It is stored in your large intestine until you go to the toilet.

Why does my heart beat?

To pump blood and oxygen around your body. Your heart is about the size of your fist and is made of muscle. When it beats, your heart squeezes blood into tubes. These carry blood and oxygen around your body. The blood then comes back to the heart from the lungs, with more oxygen.

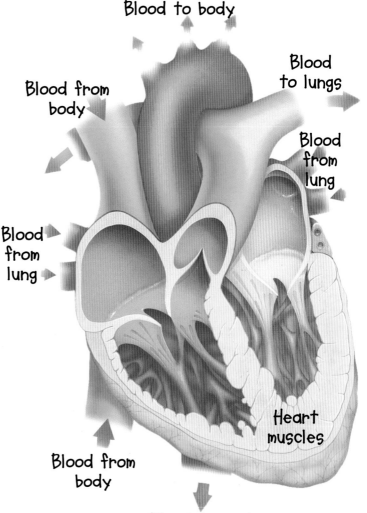

Blood to body

Blood to lungs

Blood from body

Blood from lung

Blood from lung

Blood from body

Heart muscles

Blood to body

Beat of life!

Your heart beats once a second for the whole of your life. That is 86,000 beats a day, and 31 million beats a year. In total, this is 2000 million beats in your life.

What does blood do?

Your whole body needs oxygen to work. Blood carries oxygen to every part of your body in its red cells. Blood also contains white cells that fight germs. Tubes called arteries and veins carry blood around your body.

Artery

Red cell

Does blood get dirty?

Yes, it does. Because blood carries waste away from your body parts, it has to be cleaned. This is done by your kidneys. They take the waste out of the blood and make a liquid called urine. This liquid leaves your body when you go to the toilet.

White cell

Feel

Touch your neck under your chin. Can you feel the blood flowing through an artery to your brain?

Are my eyes like a camera?

Your eyes work like a tiny camera. They collect light that bounces off the things you are looking at. This makes tiny pictures at the back of the eyes. Here, millions of sensors pick up the light. They send a picture to your brain along a nerve.

In a spin!

Inside your ear are loops full of liquid. They can tell when you move your head. This helps you to balance. If you spin around, the fluid keeps moving. This makes you feel dizzy!

Lens collects light

Pupil lets light into your eye

Nerve to brain

Muscles make eye move

What is inside my ears?

The flap on your head is only part of your ear. The hole in your ear goes to a tiny piece of tight skin, called an eardrum. Sounds enter your ear and make the eardrum move in and out. Tiny bones pass these movements to the cochlea, which is shaped like a snail. This is filled with liquid.

Look

Look in the mirror at your eye. Can you see the dark pupil where light goes in?

Ear bones

Cochlea

Ear drum

Ear flap

How do I hear sounds?

The cochlea in your ear contains thousands of tiny hairs. It is also is full of liquid. Sounds make the liquid move. This makes the hairs wave about. Tiny sensors pick up the waving, and send messages to your brain so you hear the sound.

Why can't I see smells?

Because they're invisible! Smells are tiny particles that float in the air. Inside the top of your nose are sticky smell sensors. When you sniff something, the sensors collect the smell particles. They send messages to your brain, which tell you what you can smell.

Smell sensors

Nose

Bone

A blocked dose!
Smell and taste work together when you eat. Your sense of smell helps you to taste flavours in food. When you have a cold, your smell sensors get blocked, so you cannot taste, either.

How do I taste things?

With your tongue. Your tongue is covered with tiny taste sensors. These are called taste buds. Buds on different parts of your tongue can sense different tastes, or flavours. Your tongue also moves food around your mouth and helps you to speak.

Salty flavours are tasted here

Sour flavours are tasted here

Sweet flavours are tasted here

How many smells can I sense?

Your nose can sense about 3000 different smells. You don't just have a sense of smell so you can smell nice things, such as flowers and perfumes! Your sense of smell warns you if food is rotten before you eat it.

Think

Look at the picture of the tongue. Can you think of three different things that taste sour, sweet and salty?

Is my brain really big?

Your brain is about the same size as your two fists put together. It is the place where you think, remember, feel happy or sad – and dream. Your brain also takes information from your senses and controls your body. The main part is called the cerebrum.

Cerebrum

Right and left!

The main part of your brain is divided into two halves. The right half helps you to play music and to draw. The left half is good at thinking.

Cerebellum controls muscles

Brain stem

Can my brain really wave?

Well, sort of! Your brain works using electricity. It has about 10,000 million tiny nerve cells. Tiny bursts of electricity are always jumping around between the cells. Doctors can see your brain working by looking at the electricity with a special machine called an EEG. It shows the electricity as waves on a screen.

Remember

Your brain controls the five senses — smelling, tasting, touching, hearing — can you remember your fifth sense?

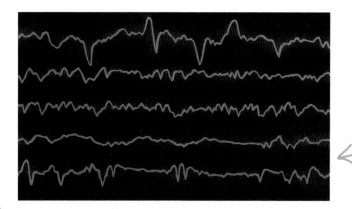

Brain waves from an EEG machine

How does my brain help me to play?

Different parts of your brain do different jobs. One part senses touch. Another part deals with thinking. Speaking is controlled by a different part. The cerebellum controls all your muscles. When you play and run, the cerebellum sends messages to your muscles to make them move.

How can I stay healthy?

There are things you can do to stop getting ill. The easiest thing is to eat the right food your body needs, such as fruit and vegetables. Try not to eat too much food. Exercise such as riding a bike will keep your bones, muscles and heart healthy.

Getting old!

Your body changes as you get old. You get shorter, your skin wrinkles and your hair might go grey. But you could live to be 100!

What can make me sick?

Lots of things can make you sick. Illnesses such as tummy upsets are caused by germs that get into your body. You can help to stop catching germs by washing your hands before eating and after going to the toilet.

Washing your hands kills germs

Why do I have injections?

All children have injections at the doctors every few years. The injections help to stop you catching serious diseases in the future. Doctors also help you to get well again when you are ill. The doctor might give you medicine to make you feel better.

Riding a bike can keep you healthy

Read

Read this page again. What should you do before meal times and after going to the toilet?

Quiz time

Do you remember what you have read about your body? These questions will test your memory. The pictures will help you. If you get stuck, read the pages again.

3. How much hair do I have?

page 194

4. How are bones joined together?

page 197

page 191

1. Am I always learning?

page 198

5. How do muscles work?

page 193

2. Why do I sweat when I'm warm?

page 201

6. What makes air go into my lungs?

7. Why do I need to eat food?

page 203

11. How do I taste things?

page 211

8. How many sets of teeth do I have?

page 204

12. How does my brain help me to play?

page 213

9. What does blood do?

page 207

13. What can make me sick?

page 215

Answers

1. Yes, you are
2. To help you cool down again
3. You have five million hairs on your body
4. They are connected by joints
5. The fibres inside get shorter and pull
6. Muscles
7. To keep your body working
8. Two sets
9. Carries oxygen around your body
10. With the parts that are inside your ear
11. With your tongue
12. It tells your muscles to move
13. Germs

page 209

10. How do I hear sounds?

Questions about...

What is a dinosaur?	220
When did dinosaurs live?	220
Where did the dinosaurs live?	221

Did any dinosaurs eat plants?	222
Why were dinosaurs so big?	223
Why did dinosaurs eat stones?	223
How big is a dinosaur tooth?	224
Did plant eaters need	
sharp teeth?	224
Did all dinosaurs have teeth?	225

What were the biggest dinos?	226
What was the biggest dinosaur	
that ever lived?	227
What did sauropods eat?	227
Why did dinosaurs have claws?	228
Were all claws sharp?	229
Which dinosaur had a spike	
on each hand?	229
What was the scariest dinosaur?	230
What was the biggest	
meat-eating dinosaur?	231
How did meat eaters get	
their food?	231
Which dinosaur had big eyes?	232
What were the noisiest	
dinosaurs?	233
Were dinosaurs clever or stupid?	233

Dinosaurs

Did dinosaurs live alone?   240
Could dinosaurs leap and jump?   241
Why are some dinosaurs
   like birds?   241

Why did the dinosaurs die?   242
What killed millions of animals?   243
Could the dinosaurs have died
   from a disease?   243

How fast could dinosaurs move?   234
Could big dinosaurs move quickly?   235
Were some dinosaurs small?   235

Did dinosaurs wear armour?   236
Which dinosaur had a lumpy tail?   237
Which dinosaur had three horns?   237

How did dinosaurs have babies?   238
Did dinosaurs look after their
   babies?   239

How do we
know about
dinosaur
babies?   239

Can we find new dinosaurs?   244
Where do scientists find dinosaur
   fossils?   245
Could dinosaurs ever come
   back to life?   245

Quiz time   246

What is a dinosaur?

Dinosaurs were animals that lived millions of years ago. There were lots of different types of dinosaur – little ones, big ones, fierce ones and shy ones. All dinosaurs lived on land – and they died out a long time ago. There are no dinosaurs living today.

Make

Use salt dough or plasticine to make some dinosaur models. Use a picture or a toy dinosaur as a guide.

When did dinosaurs live?

It is thought that the first dinosaurs lived around 230 million years ago. They roamed the Earth for the next 165 million years, before becoming extinct (dying out) about 65 million years ago. Humans haven't been around for two million years yet!

Herrerasaurus

Where did the dinosaurs live?

Dinosaurs lived all over the world. At that time, the weather was much hotter than it is today. There were plants such as ferns, mosses and large evergreen trees, but there were no flowers.

What a terror!

The word 'dinosaur' means 'terrible lizard', even though dinosaurs weren't lizards! Many of the plant-eating dinosaurs were about as terrible as today's sheep!

Did any dinosaurs eat plants?

Many dinosaurs ate plants. *Plateosaurus* grew up to 8 metres long. It had a long neck and could reach high up into trees by standing on its back legs. It grabbed branches with the hooks on its thumbs and nibbled at the tastiest leaves.

Plateosaurus

List
Starting with the letter A, list plants that you eat. A could be for apple, B for banana and C for carrot.

Why did dinosaurs eat stones?

Lots of plant-eating dinosaurs swallowed their food without chewing. Instead, they gobbled stones and pebbles, which stayed in their stomachs. When they swallowed food, the stones helped to mash the food up, turning it into a pulp.

No fruit!

Early plant-eating dinosaurs did not eat fruit or grass — none had appeared yet! Instead, they ate plants called horsetails, ferns, cycads and conifer trees.

Why were dinosaurs scaly?

Like reptiles today, such as crocodiles and alligators, dinosaurs were covered in super-tough scaly skin. The scales would have protected a dinosaur against the teeth and claws of enemies and the bites of pests such as mosquitoes and flies.

Tyrannosaurus rex

How big is a dinosaur tooth?

Dinosaur teeth were different sizes. Meat eaters, such as *Tyrannosaurus rex*, needed large, sharp and pointed teeth for tearing flesh. Each tooth measured up to 15 centimetres! When scientists look at dinosaur teeth they can work out what type of food the dinosaur ate.

Toothy!

Baryonyx had small, pointed, cone-shaped teeth. These are like the teeth of a crocodile or dolphin today. They were good for grabbing slippery food such as fish.

Did plant eaters need sharp teeth?

Plant-eating dinosaurs, such as *Apatosaurus*, had long, thin teeth that were blunt, not sharp. They used these teeth to pull leaves off branches. Herds of these dinosaurs could strip all the plants clean in one area, before moving on.

Tyrannosaurus rex fossil

Think
You have different types of teeth. Think about which ones you use to cut food, and which ones you use to chew.

Did all dinosaurs have teeth?

Not all dinosaurs needed teeth. *Ornithomimus* had a beak-shaped mouth without teeth. Its mouth was made from the same tough substance as our hair and nails. This bird-like dinosaur probably pecked at seeds, worms and bugs. Its large eyes helped it to find food.

Ornithomimus

What were the biggest dinos?

The biggest dinosaurs, called sauropods, were ENORMOUS! Each one could weigh as much as ten elephants. *Brachiosaurus* was one of the largest dinosaurs that ever lived and was 25 metres long. It was twice as tall as a giraffe and could reach the tops of the tallest trees.

Brachiosaurus

Draw

Lots of animals eat plants and live in groups, or herds. Draw some modern animals that spend all day eating plants.

Argentinosaurus

What was the biggest dinosaur that ever lived?

The biggest dinosaur ever discovered is *Argentinosaurus*. Not much is known about this giant, but it is thought that it may have measured 40 metres from head to tail! *Argentinosaurus* had a huge body but a small head and brain.

Scary tail!

Diplodocus is also known as 'Old Whip–tail'! It could swish its tail so hard that it made a CRACK! like a whip. This would scare off enemies or even rip off their skin.

What did sauropods eat?

All sauropods ate plants. They probably had to spend most of the day eating, just to get enough energy for their enormous, heavy bodies. They may have spent 20 hours every day just grazing and nibbling at plants.

Why did dinosaurs have claws?

Most dinosaurs had claws on their fingers and toes. Meat-eating dinosaurs, such as *Deinonychus* (die-non-ee-kus) used their claws for catching and killing other animals. These dinosaurs were fast, clever and strong. Their claws could cut like knives and their teeth were razor-sharp.

Discover

Look at books to find pictures of elephants' feet. Do their toenails look like the claws of Apatosaurus?

Deinonychus

Apatosaurus

Claws

Were all claws sharp?

Even plant-eating dinosaurs, such as sauropods, had claws. They didn't need claws to catch other animals, so they were flat and blunt rather than sharp. *Apatosaurus* had claws to protect its feet from stones, just like nails protect your fingertips and toes.

Thumb nose!

When scientists discovered remains of *Iguanodon*, they found a bone shaped like a horn. They put this on *Iguanadon's* nose. Now they think it is a thumb claw!

Which dinosaur had a spike on each hand?

Iguanodon was a plant-eating dinosaur. It didn't need spikes to kill other animals, but it could use them as weapons to defend itself. If meat-eating dinosaurs attacked *Iguanodon*, it could fight back with its strong arms, using its spikes like daggers.

What was the scariest dinosaur?

Tyrannosaurus rex – known as *T-rex* for short – is one of the scariest dinosaurs. This dinosaur was a large meat eater. It had powerful legs that helped it run fast and a huge mouth filled with lots of sharp, pointed teeth.

Tyrannosaurus rex

Colour

No one knows what colour dinosaurs were. Draw your favourite dinosaur, then colour it in using spots, stripes and colours!

Giganotosaurus

What was the biggest meat-eating dinosaur?

Giganotosaurus was even bigger than *T-rex* — it is the largest meat-eating dinosaur ever found. Its huge legs could carry more than 8 tonnes of weight, even when it was chasing its prey. It had small arms and both had three claws for grabbing and stabbing.

How did meat eaters get their food?

Some meat eaters hunted and captured their prey using their powerful claws and sharp teeth. Others were scavengers. This means that they ate any dead animals that they found. It is thought that *T-rex* both hunted, and scavenged, for food.

Bite marks!

Some meat-eating dinosaurs not only bit their prey, but also each other! Remains of a T-rex had bite marks on its head. Perhaps the dinosaurs fought each other to become leader of the pack.

Which dinosaur had big eyes?

Dinosaurs used their senses to see, touch, hear, smell and taste. *Troodon* was a bird-like dinosaur that had HUGE eyes. Scientists think it may have hunted at night, and that its large eyes helped it to find food in the dark.

Troodon

Play
Play a game of hide and seek. Use your senses, such as seeing and hearing, to hunt your prey!

What were the noisiest dinosaurs?

We can't be sure what sounds dinosaurs made, but *Parasaurolophus* was probably one of the noisiest! It had a large crest on its head that was made of hollow bone. *Parasaurolophus* could have blown air through the crest to make a bellowing noise, like a giant trumpet.

Were dinosaurs clever or stupid?

Animals with big brains are usually cleverer than those with small brains. *Apatosaurus* had a tiny brain. *Troodon* had a large brain, compared to the size of its body. It may have been one of the cleverest dinosaurs that ever lived.

Dino rap!

Small meat-eating dinosaurs are called 'raptors'. These dinos lived and hunted in packs. They were slim, clever and fast. Some even had feathers to keep them warm!

How fast could dinosaurs move?

Some dinosaurs could run very fast – up to 80 kilometres an hour. That is faster than a horse at full gallop! *Ornithomimus* could run this fast because it had a slim body, hollow bones and long, thin legs. It ran fast so it could chase other animals, and escape being eaten itself!

Ornithomimus

Print

Dip feathers in paint and press them on paper to make your own prints. Try making handprints, too.

Could big dinosaurs move quickly?

Large dinosaurs were often slower. Heavy bodies were harder to move! *Muttaburrasaurus* was a big dinosaur that may have run on its hind legs, holding its head up to look for enemies. Its long tail may have helped it to keep its balance.

Muttaburrasaurus

Speedy!

Coelophysis (co–el–off–ee–sis) could trot, jump and leap. It ran upright on its two back legs. It could also bound along on all four legs like a dog, at speeds of 30 kilometres an hour.

Were some dinosaurs small?

All dinosaurs were quite small when they first hatched from their eggs! Some fully-grown dinosaurs were not much bigger than a pet cat. *Compsognathus* was a small, light dinosaur that ate little creatures, such as lizards and bugs.

Did dinosaurs wear armour?

Dinosaurs needed to protect themselves from their enemies. Some of them did this by growing great pieces of bone over their bodies. These bony plates protected the dinosaurs' soft bodies underneath, like huge shields, or suits of armour.

Triceratops

Which dinosaur had a lumpy tail?

Euoplocephalus (you-o-plo-seff-a-lus) had a tail that was strengthened with lumps of bone. When this dinosaur swung its tail, it could hit an attacker with such force that it could break a leg!

Blink!

The armoured dinosaur Euoplocephalus (you–oh–ploh–sef–al–us) was so well–protected that it even had bony plates on its eyelids, which could snap open and closed, just like shutters!

Which dinosaur had three horns?

Triceratops was a plant eater and it probably used its three horns to frighten away attackers. It would also have used them for fighting enemies. *Triceratops* looked scary, but it probably spent most of its time quietly eating plants.

Styracosarus

Euoplocephalus

Protoceratops

Make

Make a dinosaur model from clay or dough and then add a suit of armour. Include horns and a tail-club, using cardboard or pebbles.

How did dinosaurs have babies?

Dinosaurs laid eggs, just like birds, lizards and crocodiles do today. *Protoceratops* was a small dinosaur, the size of a pig. It lived in the desert. The female made a bowl-shaped nest in the warm sand and then laid her eggs inside it.

Find out

Find out how much you weighed and how long you were when you were born. Ask how quickly you grew!

Did dinosaurs look after their babies?

Some dinosaurs did look after their babies, until they were old enough to look after themselves. *Maiasaura* collected food for its newly hatched young and fed it to them, rather like birds feed their chicks today. The parents probably guarded their babies, too.

Maiasaura   Baby dinosaurs

Protoceratops

How do we know about dinosaur babies?

Scientists have found dinosaur eggs, and the remains of nests that have lasted for millions of years. They have even discovered large areas where many *Maiasaura* mothers came to lay their eggs, year after year.

Big baby!

Baby dinosaurs grew up to five times faster than human babies! A baby dinosaur, such as Diplodocus, was already one metre long and 30 kilograms in weight when it came out of its egg!

Did dinosaurs live alone?

Some dinosaurs lived alone, but many lived in groups, or herds. *Velociraptor* was a fast runner and meat eater that lived in packs. Just like today's lions and wolves, *Velociraptor* could kill bigger animals than itself. These dinosaurs hunted together.

Velociraptor

Fossil poo!

Dinosaur droppings also form fossils! These have pieces of food inside such as bones or plants. Some fossil droppings are as big as TV sets!

Coelophysis

Could dinosaurs leap and jump?

Scientists work out how dinosaurs moved by looking at their bones. The bones of *Coelophysis* are small, hollow and light so it was probably able to dart about easily. The shapes of its teeth and jaw bones suggest that *Coelophysis* ate insects or fish.

Anatosaurus

Look

Look at some pictures of birds such as ostriches. Do they remind you of any dinosaurs in this book?

Why are some dinosaurs like birds?

Some dinosaurs had feathers, large eyes and beaks. They even laid eggs and ate insects. It is believed that some changed (evolved) over time and became the very first birds on Earth.

Why did the dinosaurs die?

About 65 million years ago the dinosaurs suddenly died (became extinct). No one knows for sure why this happened, but something HUGE must have taken place to affect all life on the planet.

The dinosaurs may have been killed by a giant rock from space

Read

Go to the library to find out about animals today that are in danger of becoming extinct. Find out why.

What killed millions of animals?

Maybe volcanoes erupted, spitting out enormous clouds of ash and poisonous gas. Maybe a large lump of rock from space (a meteorite) smashed into the Earth. These things can change the weather, so perhaps the dinosaurs died because it got too cold for them.

Erupting volcanoes

Egg hunters!

Some dinosaurs might have become extinct because their eggs were eaten by other animals. Shrew–like creatures around at the time may have eaten the eggs at night as dinosaurs slept.

Could the dinosaurs have died from a disease?

This is unlikely because it wouldn't explain why so many millions of other animals died too. It is thought that more than two-thirds of all living things died at the same time as the dinosaurs, including sea creatures and plants.

Can we find new dinosaurs?

The remains of animals and plants that lived long ago are called fossils. These remains are bones, teeth, eggs and footprints – that have turned to rock over millions of years. Fossils of new dinosaurs such as *Jobaria* and *Janenschia* have been found in Africa.

Jobaria

Think

If you found fossils from a new dinosaur, think of what name you would give your own dinosaur.

Leaellynasaura

Janenschia

Where do scientists find dinosaur fossils?

Fossils are difficult to find because they are usually buried deep underground. Scientists look in places where layers of rock and soil have been removed by wind or water. At Dinosaur Cove the sea has washed away the rock, revealing the fossils of *Leaellynasaura*.

Could dinosaurs ever come back to life?

It is unlikely that dinosaurs will ever walk the Earth again. However, scientists are still finding fossils and using them to uncover new facts about the lives of these magnificent creatures. Dinosaurs live on, but only in our imaginations!

Quiz time

Do you remember what you have read about dinosaurs? These questions will test your memory. The pictures will help you. If you get stuck, read the pages again.

3. What were the biggest dinos?

page 226

4. What was the scariest dinosaur?

page 230

page 223

1. Why did dinosaurs eat stones?

5. What was the biggest meat-eating dinosaur?

page 231

2. How big is a dinosaur tooth?

page 224

6. Which dinosaur had big eyes?

page 232

7. Were some dinosaurs small?

page 235

11. Why did the dinosaurs die?

page 242

8. Which dinosaur had a lumpy tail?

page 237

12. Where do scientists find dinosaur fossils?

page 245

13. Could dinosaurs ever come back to life?

page 245

9. Did dinosaurs look after their babies?

page 239

10. Could dinosaurs leap and jump?

page 241

Answers

1. To mash food up in their stomachs
2. Different sizes
3. Sauropods
4. Tyrannosaurus rex
5. Giganotosaurus
6. Troodon
7. Yes, some were not much bigger than pet cats
8. Euoplocephalus
9. Yes, some did
10. Yes, Coelophysis could
11. Volcanoes may have erupted, or a meteorite may have smashed into the Earth
12. In rocks
13. No

Questions about...

Are all bugs insects?   250
How many wings does
   an insect have?   251
Do insects have skeletons?   251

Where do butterflies come from? 252
How far can a flea jump?   253
Which butterfly flies the highest? 253

Why are butterflies
   brightly coloured?   254
Where do cockroaches live?   255
Can insects walk on water?   255

Why do bees make honey?   256
How many times can
   a bee sting you?   257

Why do bees have a queen?   257

Why do spiders make silk?   258
Can spiders spit?   258
Do spiders have fangs?   259

Why do crickets chirp?   260
What is a termite?   261
Which insect can eat a house?   261

Which insect is a flying hunter? 262
Do insects like to pray?   263
Can insects spread disease?   263

Bugs

Why are scorpions' tails
   so deadly?   264
Which beetle carries a
   spray gun?   265
What is the deadliest spider?   265

Why are there spiders in
   the bath?   266
When is a hornet not a hornet?   267
Can ants join the army?   267

Why do ladybirds have spots?   268
Which insect glows at night?   269
Can beetles dive?   269

Why do ants cut up leaves?   270
Why do moths like the moonlight?   271
Which spider looks like a crab?   271

Which bug has the most legs?   272
What are the greediest insects?   273
Can spiders change colour?   273

Do earwigs really live in ears?   274
How do insects help flowers
   to grow?   275
Where do insects spend winter?   275

Quiz time   276

Are all bugs insects?

Garden spider is an arachnid

Insects are the largest of all the animal groups. There are millions of different kinds that live almost everywhere in the world. Not all bugs are insects. Spiders belong to a group called arachnids, and millipedes are in yet another group called myriapods.

Pill millipede is a myriapod

Ladybird is an insect

Dinner date!

Breeding time is very dangerous for the praying mantis. After mating, the female may eat the male.

How many wings does an insect have?

Most insects have two pairs of wings and they use them to fly from place to place. A large moth flaps its wings once or twice each second, whilst some tiny flies flap their wings almost 1000 times each second.

Do insects have skeletons?

Insects do not have a bony skeleton inside their bodies like we do. Instead, their bodies are covered by a series of horny plates. This is called an exoskeleton.

Moth

Look

Have a look in your garden, under rocks and in the soil. How many different insects can you find?

Where do butterflies come from?

① Caterpillar hatches from an egg

Butterflies start off life as caterpillars – wriggly grubs that hatch from eggs. Caterpillars eat lots of leaves, and when they are big enough, they attach themselves to twigs. They form hard shells called pupas. Inside the pupa, the caterpillar changes into a butterfly. When the butterfly is fully formed, it breaks out of its pupa.

② Pupa is formed

③ Butterfly breaks out of its pupa

Fast mover!

The green tiger beetle is a fast-moving hunter that races over open ground. It chases smaller creatures such as ants, woodlice, worms and spiders.

④ Butterfly
flies away

Peacock
butterfly

Paint

Fold some paper in half.
Open it up and paint two
butterfly wings on one
side. Fold it again and
open it up to see all of
the butterfly.

How far can a flea jump?

Fleas can jump a very long distance
for their body size. These tiny insects
measure just 2 to 3 millimetres in
length. They can jump over
30 centimetres, which is more
than 100 times their body size.

Flea

Which butterfly flies the highest?

One of the strongest insect
fliers is the Apollo butterfly.
It can fly high over hills
and even mountains, then
it rests on a rock or
flower in the sunshine.

Why are butterflies brightly coloured?

Like many butterflies, the monarch butterfly has bright, bold colours on its wings. These warn other animals, such as birds and lizards, that it tastes horrible and is not good for them to eat.

Tasty treats!

Animal droppings are delicious to many kinds of insects. Various beetles lay their eggs in dung. The young insects then hatch out and eat it.

Where do cockroaches live?

Just about everywhere! Cockroaches are beetles that run quickly across the ground. They have low, flat bodies and can dart into small spaces under logs, stones and bricks. They can also hide in cupboards, furniture – and beds!

Cockroach

Monarch butterfly

Think

Write a list of any fast-running animals that you can think of.

Can insects walk on water?

Some insects can. The pondskater has a slim, light body with long, wide legs, which allow it to glide across the surface of the water.

Why do bees make honey?

Bees make sweet, sticky honey packed with energy. Wild bees make honey to feed themselves and their growing young, which are called larvae. Lots of animals eat honey, including humans, who keep honeybees in nests called hives so that the honey is easier to collect.

Honeybees

How many times can a bee sting you?

A bee can only sting once in its whole lifetime. After a bee jabs its sting into an enemy, the sting stays in its victim. As the bee flies away, the rear part of its body tears off and the bee soon dies.

Sting

Yummy!

Ants get food from insects called aphids. When an ant strokes an aphid, it oozes a drop of 'milk' called honeydew, which the ant then drinks.

Taste

Ask an adult if you can taste some honey. See if you think it tastes sweet and sticky, too.

Why do bees have a queen?

The queen bee lays all of the eggs, from which young bees hatch. Without her, there would be no other bees. Worker bees look after the queen and the eggs.

Why do spiders make silk?

Spiders make very thin, fine threads called silk. Some spiders use their silk to make webs to catch their prey. Other spiders wrap up their victims in silk to stop them escaping. Female spiders make silk bags called cocoons and lay their eggs in them.

Can spiders spit?

The spitting spider can. It feeds on mosquitoes, moths and flies. When it spots its prey, it spits a sticky silk thread over it. This stops the victim moving, so the spider can eat it.

Find

See if you can find a spider's web. Look in the corners of windows, in garages and in sheds.

fly stuck in web

Spider
on its web

Do spiders have fangs?

Spiders have sharp fangs in their jaws,
which they use to grab and bite their
prey. The fangs inject a poison to kill
the victim. The spider then
eats its food by
sucking out the
body juices.

Crowded house!

A wasps' nest may have
about 2000 wasps in
it, but a termite
colony may have over
five million termites.

Why do crickets chirp?

Cricket →

Male crickets chirp to attract the attention of female crickets. Their wings have hard, ridged strips at the base like a row of pegs, which make a chirping sound when they are rubbed together.

Pretend

Make your own insect noise and pretend to be an insect. Can you chirp like a cricket?

What is a termite?

Termites are small insects that are similar to ants. They live in large groups called colonies, which include king, queen, worker and soldier termites. Soldier termites protect the rest of the colony and have large jaws that they use as weapons.

Soldier termite

Worker termite

Fantastic flies!

In winter, flies die from cold and hunger. Before they die, they lay eggs in sheltered places so that next year new flies will hatch.

Which insect can eat a house?

Termites can damage wooden houses by making their nests inside the wood. The damage cannot be seen from the outside until the wood is almost hollow. If anyone touches it, the house might collapse.

Which insect is a flying hunter?

Dragonflies are fierce flying hunters. Their huge eyes spot tiny prey such as midges and mayflies. They dash through the air and use their legs to catch their victims. Then they fly back to their perch to eat their meal.

Dragonfly

Do insects like to pray?

The praying mantis is named because its front legs are folded, as if it is praying. In fact, it is waiting to grab some food. It waits for a fly or moth to come near, then SNAP! It grabs the victim very quickly with its front legs.

Praying mantis

Remember

Can you remember what dragonflies like to eat? Read these pages again to find out.

Can insects spread disease?

Many insects spread germs and disease. The mosquito is one of the deadliest. In hotter parts of the world, when it bites people to suck their blood, it may pass on a terrible illness such as malaria or yellow fever.

Playing dead!

When in danger, the click beetle falls onto its back and pretends to be dead. When the danger has gone, it arches its body and then straightens out with a jerk and a 'click'!

Why are scorpions' tails so deadly?

Scorpions have poisonous stings at the end of their tails. They use them to attack their victims. Scorpions may also wave their tails at enemies to warn them that, unless they go away, they will sting them to death!

Scorpion

Which beetle carries a spray gun?

The bombardier beetle squirts out a spray of smelly liquid from its rear end, almost like a small spray gun! This startles and stings an attacker and gives the beetle time to escape.

Discover

Spiders and scorpions belong to the same family group. Try and find out what the group is called.

Scary spiders!

The name 'tarantula' was first given to a type of wolf spider from Europe. Tarantulas are the biggest type of spider and live in hot parts of the world.

Black widow spider

What is the deadliest spider?

Black widow spiders are the most feared and dangerous of all spiders. They are small, shiny and black and they have a poisonous bite that can kill people. After mating, the female black widow spider may eat the male.

265

Why are there spiders in the bath?

Hornet

House spider

House spiders don't go in the bath to get clean. They hunt at night, and may slide into a bath by accident. The sides of the bath are too steep and slippery for them to climb out.

When is a hornet not a hornet?

The hornet-moth looks similar to a large type of wasp known as a hornet. This wasp has a very painful sting, but the hornet-moth is harmless. However, few other creatures dare to eat it as they think it is a wasp.

Hornet-moth

Grow up!

The American cicada is a kind of grasshopper. Its young live underground and they can take 17 years to change into adults!

Can ants join the army?

Ants don't really join the army. Army ants, travel in large groups of about 10,000 insects. They crawl in long lines through the forest, eating whatever they can bite and overpower, including spiders, lizards and birds.

Play

With a group of friends, get in a line and march around like a group of army ants.

Why do ladybirds have spots?

Ladybirds have bright pink, yellow or red bodies that are covered in black spots. These bright colours and spots tell other animals not to eat them, as they don't taste very nice.

Ladybird

268

Which insect glows at night?

Fireflies are not flies but a type of beetle. They produce a green or yellow light from their stomachs to attract a partner. Fireflies live on plants and trees during the day and are only active at night.

Firefly →

Think

Can you name any other insects or animals that have spots?

Sticking around!

Stick and leaf insects look exactly like sticks and leaves. When the wind blows, they rock and sway in the breeze like real twigs and leaves.

Can beetles dive?

Yes, beetles can dive. The great diving beetle lives in ponds and lakes and is a fast and fierce hunter. It uses its legs like paddles to dive through the water and catch its food.

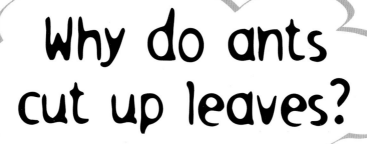

Why do ants cut up leaves?

Leafcutter ants cut up small sections of leaves to take back to their nests. The ants then carry the leaves back to a special 'ant' garden where they are stored and used as food for the ants.

Tough bug!

The young of the cranefly or 'daddy long-legs' is called a leather jacket after its tough skin.

Why do moths like the moonlight?

Most moths, such as the Indian moon moth, like moonlight. They use it to search for plant juices such as nectar in flowers. By day they rest in cracks in rocks or among leaves.

Moon moth

Which spider looks like a crab?

Crab spiders look like small crabs with wide bodies and curved legs. They sit on flowers and lie in wait for small insects to grab and eat.

Leafcutter ants

Think

Do you know of any other animals that become active after dark?

Which bug has the most legs?

Centipedes are long and thin, and usually have more than 30 legs. There are more than 3000 types of centipede. Millipedes are even longer and may have up to 100 legs.

Centipede

Millipede

Draw
Use brightly coloured pens or pencils and draw your very own crab spider.

What are the greediest insects?

Locusts are a type of grasshopper. They live in dry, warm places. If locusts find a field of crops, they swoop down in large swarms and begin to feast. The whole field can be gone in less than an hour.

Thorny tail

The thorn bug has a hard, pointed body that makes it look like a thorn on a plant.

Can spiders change colour?

Crab spiders hide themselves in flowers and plants so they can catch food. They change colour to match their surroundings so that other insects can't see them. This is called camouflage.

Gold leaf crab spider →

Do earwigs really live in ears?

Earwigs don't really crawl into ears or hide in wigs. But they do like dark, damp corners. At night they come out to feed on flower petals, one of their favourite foods.

Earwig

Discover
Try to find out what other animals migrate when the weather gets colder.

274

How do insects help flowers to grow?

Many insects, including butterflies, visit flowers to collect nectar and pollen. They carry the pollen from flower to flower. This helps flowers form seeds or fruits so that new plants can grow.

Painted lady butterfly

Where do insects spend winter?

Some insects travel to warmer lands when the weather gets cold. This is called migration. In North America, monarch butterflies fly south during autumn. They spend the winter in warmer parts of America and fly north again in the spring.

Wonderful webs!

A web-spinning spider makes a new web almost every night – eating the old one to recycle (use again) the silk threads.

Quiz time

page 255

Do you remember what you have read about insects and spiders? These questions will test your memory. The pictures will help you. If you get stuck, read the pages again.

3. Can insects walk on water?

page 257

4. How many times can a bee sting you?

page 258

page 251

1. How many wings does an insect have?

5. Can spiders spit?

6. Do insects like to pray?

page 253

2. How far can a flea jump?

page 263

7. Can insects spread disease?

page 263

11. Why do moths like the moonlight?

page 271

8. Why are scorpions' tails so deadly?

page 264

12. Which spider looks like a crab?

page 271

9. What is the deadliest spider?

page 272

page 265

13. Which bug has the most legs?

10. Why do ladybirds have spots?

page 268

Answers

1. Two pairs of wings
2. Over 30 centimetres
3. Yes, the pondskater can
4. A bee can only sting once
5. Yes, the spitting spider can
6. The praying mantis folds its front legs as if it is praying
7. Yes, the mosquito can pass on malaria
8. Their tails have poisonous stings
9. The black widow spider
10. To tell other animals not to eat them
11. It helps them search for food
12. The crab spider
13. The millipede

Questions about...

What is a reptile? 280
Why do reptiles sunbathe? 280
What is an amphibian? 281

Why do frogs cross the road? 282
When do amphibians sleep? 283
Can lizards dance? 283

Why do amphibians lay eggs? 284
Where do amphibians grow up? 285
Which toad carries eggs
   on its back? 285

Where do reptiles lay
   their eggs? 286
Are reptile eggs strong? 287
Do baby crocodiles cry? 287

Are there tortoises in
   the desert? 288
Are dragons real? 289
Can a frog sit on your finger? 289

Why do lizards stick to walls? 290
Why do chameleons have
   long tongues? 290
Which reptile can fly? 291

Which lizard huffs and puffs? 292
Are lizards frilly? 293
Why do lizards show off
   their muscles? 293

Reptiles & Amphibians

Why do snakes stick out
    their tongues? 294
Can you see through a gecko? ... 295
Why can't iguanas blink? 295

Which lizard can run on
    two legs? 302
Are toads colourful? 303
Do turtles play tricks? 303

Why do snakes squeeze
    their food? 296
Can reptiles live underground? . 296
Which snake changes colour? 297

Which snake writes in the sand? . 298
Why do turtles swim so far? 299
Can snakes live in water? 299

Are frogs dangerous? 300
Can a lizard's tail fall off? 300
Why do snakes shed their skin? . 301

Do reptiles eat amphibians? 304
Are crocodiles always hungry? .. 305
Can crocodiles walk on
    their tails? 305

Quiz time 306

What is a reptile?

Python

Reptiles are cold-blooded animals. This means that they cannot control their body temperature. A reptile's skin is dry and scaly. There are four kinds of reptile – snakes and lizards, crocodiles, tortoises and turtles and the tuatara, a kind of lizard.

Why do reptiles sunbathe?

Reptiles do a lot of sunbathing! This is called basking, and they do this to get warm so that they can move about. When reptiles are cold they find it difficult to move quickly.

Discover

Next time you are on the beach, bury your legs in the sand to feel how cool it is.

What is an amphibian?

Amphibians are cold-blooded animals. Most amphibians live in or around water. The skin of an amphibian is smooth and wet. The main groups of amphibians are frogs and toads, newts and salamanders and caecilians.

Eastern newt

Head in the sand!

Some amphibians, such as the spadefoot toad, live in very hot places. If it gets too hot, the spadefoot toad buries itself in the sand to cool down!

Cane toad

Why do frogs cross the road?

When spring arrives, amphibians come out of hiding. It is time for them to have their babies. Many amphibians return to the pond or stream where they were born. This may mean a very long journey through towns or over busy roads to breeding grounds.

Frogs

When do amphibians sleep?

When the weather turns cold, amphibians often hide away. They hibernate (go into a deep sleep) under stones and logs. This means that they go to sleep in the autumn, and don't wake up until the next spring!

Mind the frog!

In some places road signs warn drivers that frogs and toads are travelling along the roads to return to their breeding grounds.

Hibernating toad

Can lizards dance?

When the sand gets too hot, the sand lizard of the African Namib Desert performs a strange dance. It lifts its legs up and down off the burning sand or lies on its stomach and raises all its legs at once!

Explore

In the autumn, have a look under some stones and logs for sleeping frogs – try not to wake them!

Why do amphibians lay eggs?

1. Frog spawn

So that their babies can hatch. Amphibians lay eggs in water. Frogs and toads lay a jelly-like string or clump of tiny eggs called spawn. Newts lay one egg at a time. Some amphibians give birth to live young that are born looking like tiny adults.

2. Tadpoles hatch

Frog spawn

Toad spawn

Look

In the spring, look carefully in a pond for frog spawn. Check it each day and you might see it hatch into tadpoles!

4. Adult frog

Danger in the air!

Frogs and toads have very good hearing. They also have good senses of taste and smell to check for signs of danger in the air around them.

Where do amphibians grow up?

Most amphibians are born and grow up in fresh water such as ponds, pools, streams and rivers. They move onto dry land when they are adults and return to water to have their babies. This is called breeding. Most amphibians completely change their appearance as they grow.

3. Froglet

Which toad carries eggs on its back?

The female South American Surinam toad carries her eggs on her back. They are put there by her mate. The eggs stay on the mother's back until they hatch.

Where do reptiles lay their eggs?

Crocodile laying eggs

Unlike amphibians, most reptiles lay their eggs on land. The eggs feed and protect the young inside them. The egg yolk provides food for the growing young. The shell protects the baby reptile from the outside world.

Good luck!

A mother reptile only looks after her babies for a short time. Then they have to look after themselves. They must learn how to look for food and shelter very quickly.

Are reptile eggs strong?

Most reptile eggs are much tougher than those of amphibians. This is because they must survive life out of the water. Lizards and snakes lay eggs with leathery shells. Crocodile and tortoise eggs have a hard shell rather like birds' eggs.

Snake with eggs

Nest

Do baby crocodiles cry?

The baby Nile crocodile makes a very high-pitched noise, as if it's crying, when it is ready to hatch. Its mother then helps the baby to hatch by gently rolling the egg in her mouth.

Remember

Can you remember the two ways that an egg helps the young reptile growing inside it?

Are there tortoises in the desert?

Yes, there are. The desert tortoise is a shy reptile that lives in the sandy deserts of North America. It spends most of its time underground in the cool sand to escape the heat of the Sun. Adult desert tortoises can survive for about a year without water.

Desert tortoise

Are dragons real?

Early explorers told tales of dragons that lived in faraway lands. It may be that these explorers had seen giant lizards such as the Komodo dragon. These huge reptiles aren't really dragons at all!

Find

The Brazilian frog lives in Brazil in South America. Can you find Brazil on a map?

It's a boy...no!

A male baby alligator will develop in a warm egg, but a female baby alligator will develop in a cooler egg. For crocodiles, it's the other way around!

Brazilian frog

Can a frog sit on your finger?

One frog could! The Brazilian frog is less than 10 millimetres long and is small enough to sit on your thumbnail! The world's tiniest reptile is a type of lizard called a gecko. This lizard is less than 20 millimetres long.

Caribbean gecko

Why do lizards stick to walls?

Geckos can climb up walls or even walk upside down on ceilings. They are able to cling on because they have five wide-spreading toes, each with sticky toe-pads, on each foot. These strong pads are covered with millions of tiny hairs that grip surfaces tightly.

Why do chameleons have long tongues?

So they can catch their dinner. The chameleon keeps very still. When a tasty fly buzzes past, the chameleon catches it by quickly shooting out its long, sticky tongue and pulling the fly into its mouth.

Chameleon

Gecko

Pretend

Look in the mirror and stick out your tongue – pretend to be a chameleon catching a fly!

Which reptile can fly?

Flying geckos have webbed feet and folds of skin along their legs, tail and sides. This means that they can fly, or glide, over short distances. They do this to either catch food, or to escape from danger.

Tight spot!

The chuckwalla lizard gets itself into tight corners. It can jam itself into a crack in a rock, then puff its body up so that enemies cannot pull it out.

Which lizard huffs and puffs?

The male anole lizard guards his home from other lizards in an unusual way. If other males come too close, he puffs out a bright red throat pouch at them. Two males may face each other with puffy throats for hours at a time!

Anole lizard

Show off!

A male newt goes to great lengths to impress a female during the mating season. He often has brightly coloured skin, which he shows off to her!

Are lizards frilly?

The frilled lizard can be! This reptile has a large flap of skin that normally lies flat around its neck. When faced with danger, it spreads this skin out to form a huge, stiff neck frill that makes it look bigger and scarier!

Frilled lizard

Why do lizards show off their muscles?

Some male agamid lizards try to impress females with a little body-building. They can be seen perched on top of rocks, doing push-ups and bobbing their heads up and down.

Think

Can you think of any other animals that have brightly coloured skin, fur or feathers?

Why do snakes stick out their tongues?

Snakes have poor hearing and eyesight. They use their tongue to 'smell' the air for food or danger by constantly flicking it in and out. Rattlesnakes can sense heat given off by their prey, even in the dark.

Rattlesnake →

Count
Try to stare at something without blinking. Count how many seconds go by before you need to blink.

Can you see through a gecko?

One African gecko has very thin skin covering its ears. If you were to look at it with its ears lined up, you would be able to see light coming through from the other side of its head!

Strong shell!

A giant tortoise is so big and strong that it can support a one tonne weight. This means that it could support a small car!

Iguana

Why can't iguanas blink?

Iguanas have very big eyes and good eyesight, but they cannot blink. Unlike humans, iguanas don't have moveable eyelids. Instead of shutting their eyes to blink, they have special clear eyelids that sweep over their eyes to clean them.

Why do snakes squeeze their food?

Some snakes, like this ratsnake, kill their prey by squeezing it. They wrap their bodies around their meal and squeeze tightly until it stops breathing. Then the snake swallows the prey whole. After a big meal, the snake will not be hungry for a long time.

Can reptiles live underground?

Some reptiles slither below the ground. In hot places, some snakes burrow down into the sand to escape the Sun's fierce heat. The caecilian burrows through the mud of its tropical homeland, searching for worms to eat.

Measure

Using a tape measure, cut a piece of string 10 metres long. How many times could a royal python wrap around you?

Which snake changes colour?

The milksnake pretends to be the coral snake by changing colour. This is because the milksnake is not dangerous to bigger animals, but the coral snake is. Predators will not try to eat the coral snake because they are afraid of being bitten.

Ratsnake

Milksnake

King of snakes!

The longest snake in the world is the royal python, which grows up to 10 metres long. It could wrap its body around a person 12 times!

297

Which snake writes in the sand?

The sidewinding viper lives in the deserts of the United States. It moves along by pushing its body sideways against the sand, leaving a series of marks that are shaped like sideways letter Js. It does this so that its belly is not on the hot sand for too long.

Sidewinding viper

Why do turtles swim so far?

To have their babies. Every two or three years, sea turtles may swim 1000 kilometres to the beaches where they hatched to lay their eggs. Sea turtles have light, flat shells so they can swim easily under water.

Sea turtle

Can snakes live in water?

The floating sea snake can. Some fish swim close to the floating sea snake's tail to avoid being eaten. When the snake fancies a snack, it swims backwards, fooling the unlucky fish into thinking its head is its tail!

Giants of the sea!

The largest turtle in the sea is called the leatherback turtle. It is 2 metres long – what a giant!

Swim

When you next go swimming, try to swim backwards like a sea snake. Ask an adult to help you.

Are frogs dangerous?

Some are! Even one lick of the poison arrow frog would make a predator very ill. Its brightly coloured skin warns enemies that it is poisonous and dangerous to eat.

Can a lizard's tail fall off?

Some lizards have detachable tails! If a hungry hunter grabs the tail of a five-lined tree skink lizard, it will be left just holding a twitching tail. The lizard can quickly run away and will grow back a new tail.

Think

Can you remember how long it takes a snake to shed all of its skin?

Poison arrow frog

Why do snakes shed their skin?

A snake's skin does not grow with its body. This means that it has to shed its old skin as it grows bigger. It can take about two weeks for a snake to shed its skin completely.

Grass snake shedding skin

Ready to burst!

A snake has to swallow food whole as it can't chew. It opens its jaws extra wide to gulp down animals much larger than itself.

Which lizard can run on two legs?

Fire-bellied toad

The crested water dragon from Asia can. In an emergency, this lizard can stand up on its back legs to run away from enemies. This is because it has large back feet and can run faster on two legs than on four over short distances.

Water dragon

Are toads colourful?

The fire-bellied toad has a bright red tummy. When it is threatened, the toad leaps away to safety, and the quick flash of red confuses its attacker and gives the frog more time to escape.

Sneaky hunters!

Crocodiles and alligators wait in shallow water for animals to come and drink, then they leap up and drag them under the water.

Play

How easy is it to sneak up on someone? See how quietly you can creep around the house without being noticed.

Do turtles play tricks?

The alligator snapper turtle looks like a rock as it lies on the ocean floor. The tip of its tongue looks like a juicy worm, which it waves at passing prey to tempt them into its jaws.

Do reptiles eat amphibians?

Some do. Most reptiles are meat eaters. The dwarf crocodile is so small that one frog is a big dinner. Frogs can jump very fast, but the dwarf crocodile snaps quickly at anything that makes a splash in the water near its jaws.

Dwarf crocodile

Are crocodiles always hungry?

After a big meal, a crocodile may not feel hungry again for a month or two. One of the most dangerous reptiles is the Nile crocodile. Each year it kills more people in Africa than lions do.

Think

How many different animals can you think of that have long, powerful tails?

Old lizard!

Some crocodiles are very old indeed. They can live to be over 100 years old. Crocodiles continue to grow throughout their lives.

Can crocodiles walk on their tails?

If they are being threatened, crocodiles can move so fast that they almost leap out of the water. This is called 'tail-walking'. Their tails are long and powerful, and they can kill with a single swipe.

Nile crocodiles

Quiz time

Do you remember what you have read about reptiles and amphibians? These questions will test your memory. The pictures will help you. If you get stuck, read the pages again.

3. Which toad carries eggs on its back?

page 285

4. Where do reptiles lay their eggs?

page 286

page 280

page 290

1. What is a reptile?

5. Why do chameleons have long tongues?

2. What is an amphibian?

6. Why do lizards show off their muscles?

page 293

page 281

11. Can a lizard's tail fall off?

page 294

page 300

7. Why do snakes stick out their tongues?

page 295

12. Which lizard can run on two legs?

page 302

8. Why can't iguanas blink?

9. Can snakes live in water?

page 299

page 305

13. Are crocodiles always hungry?

10. Are frogs dangerous?

page 300

Answers

1. A cold-blooded animal with dry and scaly skin
2. A cold-blooded animal with wet and smooth skin
3. The female South American Surinam toad
4. On land
5. So they can catch their dinner
6. So they can impress females
7. To 'smell' the air for food or danger
8. Because their eyelids do not move
9. Yes, the floating sea snakes lives in water
10. The poison arrow frog is very dangerous
11. The five-lined tree skink's tail can
12. The crested water dragon from Asia
13. No. After a big meal, a crocodile may not feel hungry for a month or two

Questions about...

What is special about birds?   310
Do birds have teeth?   310
Why do birds lay eggs?   311

How do birds fly?   312
How far can a bird fly?   312
Do all birds fly?   313

Why are some birds colourful?   314
Which birds strut around
    and coo?   315
Why do birds sing?   315

Birds

Why do birds lay eggs in nests?   316
Why are cuckoos lazy?   317
How do birds build nests?   317

How does a bird eat a snail?   322
Which bird has a
   scissor-shaped beak?   323
Why do flamingos have
   long necks?   323

Quiz time   324

What is a bird of prey?   318
How does a sea eagle catch fish?   319
Do hunting birds live
   in towns?   319

Why do woodpeckers peck?   320
How do honeyguides find
   their food?   321
Do antbirds eat ants?   321

What is special about birds?

Birds can fly, walk, run and even swim! Because they have wings, birds are able to fly to all parts of the world, from steamy rainforests to the icy Arctic. There are about 9000 different types of bird, from beautiful barn owls to giant ostriches.

Do birds have teeth?

Birds don't have teeth. Instead, they have really strong mouths that are called beaks, or bills. Sharp, pointed beaks are good for grabbing bugs and short, strong beaks are great for cracking nuts open!

Discover

Beaks and feathers are made of a special tough material. See if you can you discover what it's called.

Barn owl

The early bird!

The oldest-known bird lived about 150 million years ago. Archaeopteryx (ark-ee-op-ter-ix) had feathers and wings, but it had teeth instead of a beak.

Why do birds lay eggs?

Birds lay eggs so that their babies can grow. Baby birds are called chicks and they begin life in an egg. The eggs are kept safe in a nest until they hatch.

Song thrush

Eggs in a nest

How do birds fly?

Peregrine falcon

 Birds can fly because they have wings, powerful muscles and very light bones. Feathers also help birds move smoothly through the air. This peregrine falcon is the fastest of all animals. It can reach top speeds of 180 kilometres an hour as it swoops and dives.

How far can a bird fly?

Birds can fly very long distances. Swifts are super fliers and even eat and mate while they swoop through the clouds. When young swifts leave the nest they may fly for the next two years and travel more than 500,000 kilometres!

Count
If a bird beats its wings ten times in one second, how many times would it beat its wings in two seconds?

Do all birds fly?

All birds have wings, but not all of them fly. This speedy roadrunner lives in the desert. It can fly, but it prefers to walk or run as it looks for lizards, snakes and bugs in the sand.

Roadrunner

Swift

Hum that tune!

Hummingbirds beat their wings 50 times a second. As the wings slice through the air they make the humming noise that gives the birds their name.

Why are some birds colourful?

Birds can be big show-offs and they use bright colours to make themselves look attractive. Male birds are usually more colourful than females. When this peacock sees a female (a peahen) he displays his fine tail and shakes it, so she can admire his great beauty.

Love birds!

Great crested grebes are water birds that dance for each other. During the dance they offer each other gifts – beakfuls of water weed. Lovely!

Peacock

Which birds strut around and coo?

Male birds puff up their feathers, strut around and make cooing noises to impress the females. These cocks-of-the-rocks also dance and spread their wings to show off to the female birds. They live in the South American rainforest.

Cocks-of-the-rocks

Why do birds sing?

Birds sing to get the attention of other birds. Like their colourful feathers, they may use songs to attract mates. Some birds squawk loudly if they are being attacked. Most baby birds learn to sing by copying their parents.

Dress-up

A bird's feathers are called its plumage. Put on some bright clothes and see if anyone notices your plumage!

315

Why do birds lay eggs in nests?

Birds lay their eggs in a nest to keep them safe. Once the eggs have hatched, the little chicks stay in the nest until they have grown enough to be able to fly. These bald eagles build giant nests up to 2.5 metres across.

Bald eagle

Chicks

Why are cuckoos lazy?

Cuckoos don't bother making their own nests. Instead, they lay their eggs in other birds' nests. This way cuckoos do not have all the hard work of looking after their own chicks – other birds do it for them!

How do birds build nests?

Birds build their nests in different ways, but most of them use twigs and sticks. African weaver birds make their delicate nests using strips of leaves and grass. They knot and weave the strips together to make a cosy, safe home.

Make it

Use sticks and twigs to make a nest. Make a soft lining with grass or straw. Pop some chocolate eggs in the middle.

1. The weaver bird twists strips of leaves

2. The roof is made

Watch the birdie!

Most birds take minutes to lay an egg. The mother cuckoo can lay an egg in 9 seconds! This allows her to quickly pop it in the nest of another bird.

3. The finished nest

What is a bird of prey?

Birds of prey are hunting birds. As they soar and glide across the sky they search for animals to eat. Golden eagles have extremely good eyesight and can spot food far away. They swoop to the ground and grab rabbits and mice with their sharp claws.

Golden eagle

How does a sea eagle catch fish?

Sea eagles need good eyes and strong claws to catch a swimming fish. Each foot has a pointed hook for holding onto a slippery fish. Sea eagles take their fish to a cliff or rocky ledge where they can eat in comfort.

Sea eagle

Do hunting birds live in towns?

It's unusual to see big hunting birds such as eagles in towns. But you might see smaller ones, such as ravens. These black birds are very clever animals. They hunt mice and rats but they will eat almost any food that they can find.

Why do woodpeckers peck?

Woodpeckers peck at trees to disturb the little insects that live in the bark. They then gobble them up. These birds can also use their strong, pointed beaks to hammer at the tree until they have made a hole big enough for a nest.

Hummm, I'm hungry!

Bee hummingbirds beat their wings 200 times a second. If we used up the same amount of energy we would need to eat three times our own weight in potatoes each day!

How do honeyguides find their food?

Honeyguide

Honeyguide birds follow honey badgers to find their favourite food – delicious bee grubs! The clever birds follow the badgers when they go in search of a bee's nest. When the badger opens the nest it feeds on the honey, while the birds eat the grubs and beeswax.

Make it

Ask an adult to help you make a bird feeder. You can then hang it upside down from a tree.

Do antbirds eat ants?

Antbirds follow army ants as they march through the forest, but they don't usually eat them. The birds perch on trees as the army ants pass by, then they pounce on the other small animals and insects that come to feed on the ants.

How does a bird eat a snail?

Birds that eat snails need to get the soft body out of the hard shell. Some birds smash snails against rocks. This snail kite uses its sharp beak to cut the slimy snail away from its shell and hook it out.

Knobbly knees!

Flamingos look as if they have got back-to-front legs. Actually, what appear to be their knees are really their ankles!

Snail kite

Which bird has a scissor-shaped beak?

The beak of a skimmer is shaped like scissors. This is because the lower beak is much longer and flatter than the top beak. As it flies over water, the skimmer dips its lower beak below the surface. When it touches a fish it snaps its beak shut.

Flamingo

Why do flamingos have long necks?

Flamingos have long necks so that they can reach underwater to find their food. They use their beaks to catch tiny pink creatures called shrimps that float past. Flamingos turn pink after eating lots of these shrimps!

Remember

Can you remember what a skimmer's beak is shaped like? If you can't, read this page again to find out.

Quiz time

Do you remember what you have read about birds?
These questions will test your memory. The pictures will help you. If you get stuck, read the pages again.

3. Do all birds fly?

page 313

4. Why do birds sing?

page 315

page 311

1. Why do birds lay eggs?

5. How do birds build nests?

page 317

6. Why are cuckoos lazy?

page 312

2. How far can a bird fly?

page 317

7. What is a bird of prey?

page 318

11. How does a bird eat a snail?

page 322

12. Which bird has a scissor-shaped beak?

page 323

page 319

8. Do hunting birds live in towns?

page 320

9. Why do woodpeckers peck?

page 323

13. Why do flamingos have long necks?

10. Do antbirds eat ants?

page 321

Answers

1. So their babies can grow
2. Very long distances
3. Not all birds can fly
4. To get the attention of other birds
5. With twigs and sticks
6. Because they don't make their own nests
7. A hunting bird
8. Smaller ones do
9. To disturb insects that live in the bark
10. Yes, they eat army ants
11. The snail kite hooks it out with it's beak
12. The skimmer
13. So they can reach underwater to find their food

Questions about...

Why are some animals furry? 328
What is a joey? 329
Why do some mammals sniff
   the air? 329

What is the biggest mammal? 330
How big is an elephant? 331
What is the smallest mammal? 331

How do cheetahs run so fast? 332
Why do hares kick? 333
Which mammal is very bouncy? 333

Are mammals good swimmers? 334
Can seals breathe underwater? 334
What does a killer whale kill? 335

Mammals

Are polar bears cuddly? 336
Why are some animals white? 337
How do seals stay warm? 337

Why do wolves live in packs? 338
How many meerkats live
    together? 339
What is a group of whales
    called? 339

How big is a baby panda? 340
What are baby elephants called? 341
Which mammal has the most
    babies at a time? 341

How do tigers catch their food? 342
What do bears eat? 343
Why do dogs hunt in packs? 343

Are rhinos dangerous? 344
Why do some mammals
    have scales? 345
What is the stinkiest mammal? 345

Quiz time 346

Why are some animals furry?

Fur or hair keeps some animals warm. Animals that have fur or hair are called mammals. Fur also protects from the weather. This hairy orang-utan lives in the rainforest. She picks fruit and leaves to eat. She feeds her baby on milk.

Orang-utan

What is a joey?

A joey is a baby kangaroo. When a joey is born it is smaller than your big toe! Even though it is tiny and blind, the joey crawls all the way to its mother's pouch and climbs in. It feeds on milk from its mother.

Joey

Egg-citing news!

Most mammals give birth. This means that they have babies, cubs or kittens. Some strange mammals, such as the duck-billed platypus, lay eggs.

Find out

Were you a beautiful baby, or did you hatch from an egg? Look at old photos of yourself to find out.

Why do some mammals sniff the air?

Many mammals use their noses to get information about the world around them. Their noses are very sensitive to smells. Wild animals, such as deer and rabbits, sniff the air around them to check for signs of danger.

What is the biggest mammal?

The blue whale is – and it's enormous! In fact, it is the biggest animal that has ever lived. Even a baby blue whale is huge – it measures 7 metres in length. All whales are mammals and give birth to their babies, which are called calves.

What a hooter!

African elephants have the longest noses! Their noses are called trunks and they can be 2.5 metres long. Trunks are used for smelling, picking up food and drinking.

How big is an elephant?

One African elephant can weigh more than 100 people put together. Elephants are the biggest animals that live on land and they can reach 4 metres in height. They spend most of their day eating to keep themselves that huge!

← African elephant

Measure

Using a measuring tape, see if you can mark out how long a blue whale calf is.

Blue whale ↙

What is the smallest mammal?

The tiny hog-nosed bat is not much bigger than your thumb! Bats are the only mammals that can fly. They usually sleep during the day and come out at night to look for food.

How do cheetahs run so fast?

Cheetahs have big muscles in their legs and they can run faster than any other animal. These speedy cats run out of breath quickly. This means that the animals they're chasing, such as gazelles, often manage to escape. Cheetahs can reach speeds of 100 kilometres an hour!

Cheetah

Why do hares kick?

Hares sometimes kick out at their enemies. Other animals such as foxes try to catch hares to eat them. If the hare sees, smells or hears an enemy, it can run fast to get away, or kick out with its back legs.

Hare

Run

How fast can you run? Ask an adult to time you next time you are in the park or garden.

Whoosh!

The pronghorn deer is one of the fastest mammals in North America. It runs fast to escape from wolves, which hunt it for food.

Gazelle

Which mammal is very bouncy?

Kangaroos bounce instead of running. The red kangaroo is a champion jumper and it leaps across the dry deserts of its Australian home. It travels quickly to search for water and food, which are hard to find in a desert.

Are mammals good swimmers?

Some mammals are super swimmers! Whales, dolphins and seals have bodies that are perfectly shaped for moving through water smoothly and quickly. They have fins and tails instead of arms and legs. Whales and dolphins spend their whole lives in water.

Harp seal

Can seals breathe underwater?

No mammals can breathe underwater — not even seals, whales and dolphins. Instead, they have to take in all the air they need when they are at the surface of the water, then hold their breath. Some seals can stay underwater for an hour at a time!

Bowhead whale

Diving deep!

The Weddell seal is a daring diver. It plunges down to the deep, dark, cold water of the oceans as it hunts for fish to eat.

What does a killer whale kill?

Killer whales kill squid, fish, seals and even birds. They are strong swimmers and have sharp, pointed teeth. Killer whales can be friendly. They live in family groups and calves stay with their mothers all their lives!

Swim

You are a mammal and you can learn to swim too! Visit your local pool for some watery fun!

Are polar bears cuddly?

Polar bears may look cuddly with their thick, white fur, but they are fierce hunters. These bears live in the ice-covered lands near the North Pole. Their fur keeps them warm – they even have fur on the soles of their feet so that their toes don't get frost bite!

Polar bear →

Lots of lemmings!

A female lemming can have her first babies when she is only 14 days old. From then on, she can have as many as 12 babies every single month!

Why are some animals white?

White animals usually live in places that are covered with snow in winter. A white Arctic hare blends into the snow and hides from enemies. In summer, the snow melts and the hare grows brown fur.

Paint

Paint a snowy scene showing some animals that live in cold places, such as polar bears, seals and penguins.

How do seals stay warm?

Seals spend a lot of their time underwater in cold parts of the world. They can keep warm because they have thick layers of fat, called blubber, under their skin. Seals also have waterproof fur that stops water getting through to their skin.

Mother seal

Seal pup

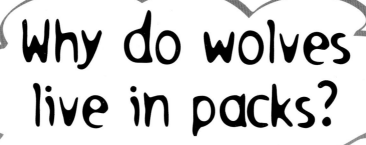

Why do wolves live in packs?

Wolves live in packs because they hunt together and look after one another. A mother wolf takes good care of her cubs. As the cubs grow, they are brought food from their father and other members of the wolf pack.

Wolves

Cool cats!

Lions may be fierce, but they are also very lazy. They sleep or doze for more than 20 hours a day, keeping cool in the shade!

How many meerkats live together?

Meerkats live in groups of up to 30 animals. A group is called a colony and each colony is made up of several families. While some meerkats search for food, others stand guard and look for enemies, such as hawks.

Meerkats ⟶

What is a group of whales called?

A group of whales is called a pod. Pilot whales live in pods of 20 or more animals that swim and hunt together. Some dolphins live in pods that may have more than 1000 members.

Count

How many people can you count in your family? Include all your grandparents, aunts, uncles and cousins.

How big is a baby panda?

Pandas give birth to tiny babies, or cubs. Each cub could fit inside your hand and weighs the same as an apple. Newborn pandas are blind and helpless. They do not open their eyes until they are two or three months old.

Panda

Panda cub

What are baby elephants called?

Baby elephants are called calves. Soon after they are born, elephant calves are able to stand up. Within a few days, they can run around. Elephants live in groups called herds. The adult elephants protect the young from lions and hyenas.

Elephant calf

Big baby!

The baby blue whale is bigger than any other mammal baby. It weighs more than 30 people put together and drinks up to 500 litres of milk every day.

Measure

How much milk do you drink every day? Use a measuring jug to see how much milk fills up a glass.

Which mammal has the most babies at a time?

The Virginia opossum can have up to 21 babies at a time – more than any other mammal. Each baby opossum is no bigger than a fingertip! If it is attacked, a Virginia opossum lies down and pretends to be dead.

How do tigers catch their food?

Tigers are hunters. Their bodies are perfect for finding, chasing and killing other animals. Stripy fur helps the tiger blend in with tall grass so they are difficult to spot. When a tiger sees a meal, it runs and pounces. It uses its claws and teeth to kill.

Tiger

Deer

What do bears eat?

Bears eat all kinds of food. Some bears hunt other animals but most eat insects, fruit and leaves. Sloth bears love to eat termites. They have long claws for digging out termite nests. The bears suck the termites up one at a time!

Great apes!

Chimpanzees live in groups that hunt together. They search for other monkeys, birds and antelopes to eat. They also form groups that attack other groups of chimpanzees.

Sloth bear

Why do dogs hunt in packs?

Wild dogs hunt in packs because they are more likely to get something to eat. By working together they can surround an animal. They may catch a bigger animal than one dog alone could catch.

Work

Working together is best. True or false? Help an adult with the shopping or the housework to find out!

Are rhinos dangerous?

A rhinoceros is one of the most dangerous mammals. Mother rhinos may attack people, or other animals, to protect their babies. They can run fast and they have sharp horns for attacking. Male rhinos also use their horns to fight one another.

Bee-eaters!

Smelly skunks sometimes feed on bees. They roll the bees on the ground to remove the stings before eating them.

Why do some mammals have scales?

Some mammals have scales to protect themselves, rather like a suit of armour. Pangolins are strange ant-eating mammals that live in Africa and Asia. Their bodies are covered in overlapping scales that protect them from other animals — and the stinging bites of ants.

Pangolin

Rhinoceros

What is the stinkiest mammal?

Skunks are very stinky mammals! These stripy creatures shake their tails at an enemy to warn it to stay away. If that doesn't work, the skunk raises its tail and sprays a smelly liquid in its enemy's face!

Make it

Ask an adult to help you make a cardboard suit of armour. How easy is it to move wearing the armour?

345

Quiz time

 Do you remember what you have read about mammals? These questions will test your memory. The pictures will help you. If you get stuck, read the pages again.

1. What is a joey?

page 329

2. What is the biggest mammal?

page 330

3. Which mammal is very bouncy?

page 333

4. Can seals breathe underwater?

page 334

5. Are polar bears cuddly?

page 336

6. Why are some animals white?

page 337

7. Why do wolves
   live in packs?

page 338

page 343

11. What do bears eat?

8. How many
   meerkats live
   together?

page 343

12. Why do
    dogs hunt
    in packs?

page 339

13. Are rhinos
    dangerous?

9. How big is a
   baby panda?

page 340

page 344

Answers

1. A baby kangaroo
2. The blue whale
3. The kangaroo
4. No
5. No, they are fierce hunters
6. To blend in with their surroundings
7. Because they hunt together and look after each other
8. Up to 30
9. As big as your hand
10. Calves
11. Insects, fruit and leaves
12. They are more likely to get something to eat
13. Yes, rhinos are one of the most dangerous animals

page 341

10. What are baby elephants called?

Questions about...

Why were the pyramids built? 350
What guards the Great Pyramid? 351
What was inside the Great
   Pyramid? 351

Who was the top god? 352
Why were cats important? 353
Who took care of the temples? 353

How were the pyramids built? 354
Were the pyramids painted white? 355
How did the workers build
   so high? 355

Ancient Egypt

How do you make a mummy?   356
What did the priest do?   357
What were mummies kept in?   357

Did food grow in the desert?   358
How did the Egyptians farm?   358
What did farmers grow?   359

Who had the best jobs?   360
Who was head of the family?   360
What did children play with?   361

Who shaved their hair off?   364
Did Egyptians ever wear wigs?   365
What was the fashion?   365

Who were the workers?   366
How did Egyptians write?   367
Did people write on paper?   367

Who had the biggest houses?   362
How did the Egyptians cook?   362
Were houses built with bricks?   363

Quiz time   368

Why were the pyramids built?

Pyramids were tombs (burial places) for Egyptian rulers, called pharaohs. The three great pyramids of Khufu, Khafre and Menkaure were built in Giza, Egypt, 4500 years ago. The Great Pyramid of Khufu is the biggest. It took 20 years and 4000 workers to build it!

Great Pyramid of Pharaoh Khufu

Pyramid of Pharaoh Khafre

Pyramid of Pharaoh Menkaure

What guards the Great Pyramid?

The pyramids were full of treasures. A stone statue was built to guard the Great Pyramid at Giza. It was carved in the shape of a sphinx. A sphinx has the body of a lion and the head of a man. The sphinx at the Great Pyramid has the face of Pharaoh Khafre.

The sphinx

Tomb robbers!

'The Book of Buried Pearls' told robbers all about the treasures inside the tombs. It also showed them how to get past spirits that guarded the dead.

What was inside the Great Pyramid?

The Great Pyramid had two huge burial chambers. They were built for the pharaoh and his queen. A corridor called the Grand Gallery led to the pharaoh's chamber. The corridor's ceiling was 8 metres tall!

Map

Draw a plan of a pyramid. Include secret tunnels and hidden rooms to stop the robbers.

Who was the top god?

Ancient Egyptians worshipped more than 1000 gods. The most important was Ra, the Sun god. Every evening, Ra was swallowed by Nut, the sky goddess. At night, Ra travelled through the land of the dead. He was born again each morning. Later, Ra became Amun Ra, king of the gods.

Ra →

Dead body god!

Anubis was the god in charge of dead bodies. He looked like a jackal, a kind of dog. People who wrapped bodies for burial often wore Anubis masks!

Why were cats important?

Cats were sacred (holy) animals in ancient Egypt. The goddess for cats, musicians and dancers was called Bastet. When a pet cat died it was wrapped up carefully and placed in a special cat-shaped coffin. Then the cat was buried in a cat cemetery!

Who took care of the temples?

Fabulous temples were built for the gods. Many temples were built for Amun Ra, king of the gods. Priests looked after the temples, their riches and the lands around them. These massive statues of Pharaoh Ramses II guard the temple at Abu Simbel.

Draw

Draw a picture of Ra travelling through the night in the land of the dead. He travelled in a boat.

Temple at Abu Simbel

How were the pyramids built?

Thousands of workers had to cut blocks of stone to the right shape using chisels and saws. Wooden sledges were then used to drag the stones to the pyramid. Each stone weighed more than two and a half big elephants!

Finished pyramid

Wooden sledge for dragging blocks

Busy busy!

One ancient Egyptian was a very busy man! Imhotep was a doctor, a priest and a poet. He also designed and built a pyramid!

Were the pyramids painted white?

The finished pyramids had a bright white coating. This wasn't paint, but limestone, which protected the stones beneath. Inner walls were built from clay bricks that were lined with pink granite. White stone covered the floors.

The pharaoh checked the work

Teams of workers dragged the stones up slopes

How did the workers build so high?

The stones were pulled up a ramp to get to each level of the pyramid. The ramp was a steep slope made from baked earth bricks. The pyramid got higher and higher. So the ramp had to be made longer and longer! Sledges were pulled up the ramp on rollers.

Think

Look at the walls and ceilings of your house. What do you think they were built with?

How do you make a mummy?

Ancient Egyptians mummified their dead. First, the inside parts such as the brain, but not the heart, were removed. Then the body was salted and dried. Cloth was stuffed inside the body to help it keep its shape. Then the body was oiled and wrapped in lots of bandages.

Mummy case

All wrapped up!

The mummy was wrapped in tight bandages. This helped to stop the body from rotting away.

The priest in charge

Mummy

Make

Cut out a mummy mask from card and paint it with a face. It could be the face of an animal.

What did the priest do?

The priest sent the dead person's spirit into the next world. He touched parts of the body with special instruments. This was so that the body could move around in the world of the dead. The mouth could speak and eat in its new life after being touched!

What were mummies kept in?

The mummy was placed in a case. Some cases were just wooden boxes. Others were beautifully decorated. An important person, such as a pharaoh, was placed in a stone coffin called a sarcophagus (sarc-off-a-gus).

Sarcophagus (sarc-off-a-gus)

Did food grow in the desert?

Most of Egypt was in the hot desert.
However, every year in July, the great
river Nile flooded the dry fields. The water
brought rich, black soil with it. This soil
spread in wide strips on each side of the
river. Farmers sowed their seed in this good soil.

Cattle were counted

How did the Egyptians farm?

Farmers used oxen and wooden ploughs to dig
the soil. They weeded and dug channels with
hoes. Then they planted seed, mostly by
hand. Farmers also kept goats, sheep, ducks
and geese. They kept bees to make honey.

Farmers' crops

What did farmers grow?

Farmers grew barley for beer and grapes for wine. Dates, figs, melons, cucumbers, onions, leeks and lettuces grew well in the rich soil. Wheat was also grown to make bread.

Farm workers

Water from the river Nile

Draw

Draw a basket full of crops grown by Egyptian farmers. You can see an Egyptian basket in this picture.

Who had the best jobs?

Doctors, high priests or priestesses and government officers had the best jobs.
So did viziers. A vizier helped the pharaoh to rule the land. Next came the traders and craftsmen, such as carpenters and jewellers. Labourers and farmhands had the poorest jobs.

Who was head of the family?

In ancient Egypt the man was the head of the family. The eldest son was given all the land, property and riches when his father died. Women could also own land and property and get good jobs.

Little monkey!

Pet baboons were sometimes trained to climb fig trees and pick the ripe fruit!

Vizier checking grain

Children playing

Imagine

Imagine you are an Egyptian worker. Which job would you choose to do and why?

What did children play with?

Children played with toys made from clay and wood. They had carved animals with legs and heads that could move. They also had spinning tops, clay balls, toy horses and dolls. Children played games such as leapfrog and tug-of-war, too.

Who had the biggest houses?

Rich family

Rich Egyptians lived in large country houses called villas.
Villas often had several storeys. Some had walled gardens with fruit orchards and a fish pond. Poor families often lived in one room. Many lived on crowded streets in the towns and cities.

How did the Egyptians cook?

Some ancient Egyptians cooked their food in a clay oven. Others cooked on an open fire. Clay ovens were made from baked clay bricks. Wood or charcoal were burned as fuel. Cooks used pottery saucepans with two handles.

Mud and straw mixture was poured into a wooden frame

Finished bricks

Were houses built with bricks?

Egyptian houses were built with bricks. Mud from the river Nile was mixed with straw and pebbles. The mixture was shaped into brick shapes and dried in the hot sun. Trunks from palm trees held up the flat roofs. Inside walls were plastered and painted.

Make

Mix clay with dried grass and pebbles. Put the mixture in an ice-cube tray. Let your bricks dry in the sun.

Sticky fingers!

Ancient Egyptians ate with their fingers. Rich people washed their hands between each dish. Their servants brought jugs of washing water for them.

Who shaved their hair off?

Both men and women shaved their hair off. They believed that this kept them clean. Men and women also wore make-up such as black kohl, which lined their eyes.

Fingernail paint and face powder were also used. Red colouring was worn on lips and cheeks.

Egyptian lady

Cosy toes!

Rich people wore shoes made with padded leather. Sandals were made of the grass-like papyrus plant. Poor people went barefoot.

Did Egyptians ever wear wigs?

Rich Egyptians wore wigs made from human hair or sheep's wool. The wigs were kept in boxes held on stands. Egyptians also used hair dye. Girls plaited their hair into pigtails. Some boys wore a pigtail on one side.

Wigs

Wooden comb

Ivory comb

Hair pins

What was the fashion?

Rich women wore the best linen cloth with beads sewn onto it. The cloth was dyed in pale colours. It was made into long dresses and cloaks. Men wore long robes. They also wore cloths wrapped around the waist. These were tied in a knot.

Make

Draw an Egyptian wearing clothes and make-up. Use wool to make a wig. Glue this to the person's head.

Who were the workers?

Most Egyptians were labourers who worked on farms and building sites. There were also carpenters, potters, jewellers and shoemakers. These people were called craftworkers and they had shops in towns. Some worked for rich people.

Craftworker

Draw
Draw symbols for different jobs. Try a hammer for a carpenter or a ring for a jeweller.

How did Egyptians write?

Egyptians used symbols for writing. These were called hieroglyphs. Some hieroglyphs stood for words. Others stood for sounds. School children had to learn 700 different hieroglyphs!

School children

Did people write on paper?

The Egyptians had no paper. Instead they wrote on papyrus. This was made from reeds that grew next to the river Nile. Papyrus lasts a long time. Sheets of it have survived 3000 years!

Packed lunch!

Workers took bread, onions and a cucumber for their lunch. They washed it down with weak beer.

Quiz time

Do you remember what you have read about Egypt?
These questions will test your memory. The pictures will help you. If you get stuck, read the pages again.

page 351

1. What guards the Great Pyramid?

page 353

2. Why were cats important?

3. What were mummies kept in?

page 357

4. What did the priest do?

page 357

5. What did farmers grow?

page 359

6. Who was head of the family?

page 360

7. What did children play with?

page 361

8. How did the Egyptians cook?

page 362

9. Who shaved their hair off?

page 364

10. What was the fashion?

page 365

11. Did Egyptians ever wear wigs?

page 365

12. Did people write on paper?

page 367

13. How did Egyptians write?

page 367

Answers

1. The sphinx
2. Because they were holy
3. Mummy case or sarcophagus
4. Sent the dead person's spirit into the next world
5. Barley, grapes, dates, figs, melons, cucumbers, onions, leeks and lettuces
6. The man
7. Wooden or clay toys, spinning tops, clay balls, toy horses and dolls
8. With clay ovens or open fires
9. Men and women
10. Dresses, cloaks and long robes
11. Rich Egyptians did
12. No, they wrote on papyrus
13. Egyptians used symbols to write

Questions about...

What was the Roman Empire?   372
Where did people go shopping?   373
Did people live in blocks of flats?   373

What did the Romans eat?   374
Did people have dinner parties?   375
Who ate takeaways?   375

What did children learn
    at school?   376
Did children use calculators?   377
Why didn't girls go to school?   377

What was a toga?   378
Did people wear make-up?   379
What were Roman hairstyles like?   379

Who wore precious jewels?   380
What was a mosaic?   381
Did people wear shoes?   381

How clean were the Romans?   382
Did the Romans listen to music?   383
What games did people play?   383

What was the Colosseum?   384
Did Romans race to the circus?   385
Was chariot racing dangerous?   385

What was army life like?   386
Was a tortoise used in battle?   387
Did soldiers cook dinner?   387

Ancient Rome

Why were roads always straight?   394
Could ships sail to Rome?   395
Did people travel in their beds? 395

What was a villa?   388
Did people keep pets?   389
Where did people go on holiday?   389

Why were farms important?   390
Did grapes grow on trees?   391
Why were olives so special?   391

Why was Rome so beautiful?   396
Were there doctors in Rome?   397
How was Rome supplied
    with water?   397

Who was the top god?   392
Did people go to church?   393
Which god started storms?   393

Quiz time   398

What was the Roman Empire?

Rome is a city in modern-day Italy. About 3000 years ago, it was just a small village. It began to grow into a large, powerful city. About 2000 years ago, Rome ruled many different lands. All of these lands, including Rome itself, were known as the Roman Empire.

Rome

Find out

The Roman Empire was huge. Try to find out which countries were part of it.

Where did people go shopping?

Rome had the world's first shopping centre. It was called Trajan's Market, and was built on five different levels on the slopes of a hill in the centre of Rome. It contained more than 150 shops in a large main hall.

Time to go!

The Romans designed the first public toilets. Users sat next to each other on rows of seats.

Did people live in blocks of flats?

The Romans built the world's first high-rise flats. Most people who lived in Ostia, a busy town close to Rome, lived in blocks of flats known as 'insulae'. Each block had up to 100 small rooms.

Blocks of flats

What did the Romans eat?

People ate just bread and fruit for breakfast. Lunch might be leftovers from the night before. The main meal was eaten in the evening. It might include meat such as goose or hare, and vegetables and fruit. It took all day to prepare.

Preparing dinner

Plan

Find out what the Romans ate then plan your own Roman menu. Include a starter, main dish and dessert.

Did people have dinner parties?

Yes, they did – and they lay down to eat! People lay on long couches around a table. They often wore crowns of flowers and they took off their sandals before entering the dining room.

Dinner party

Yuk!
Yummy dishes for a Roman banquet might include eel, thrush, dormouse or poached snails. If that upset people's stomachs, pickled cabbage was eaten to make them feel better!

Who ate takeaways?

Ordinary people did. Many went to cheap eating houses for their main meal, or bought ready-cooked snacks from roadside fast-food stalls.

What did children learn at school?

Only boys went to school. At the age of six they began to learn reading, writing, arithmetic, history and sport. They were also taught public speaking.

At school

Inky fingers!

Soot from wood fires was used to make ink. It was mixed with vinegar and sticky gum that oozed from trees. Some Roman writing has survived 2000 years.

Did children use calculators?

Calculators hadn't been invented, so children learned to count with their fingers! A wooden counting frame called an abacus was used to work out sums.

Count

If boys started school aged 6 and left when they were 16, how many years did they study for?

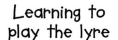

Learning to play the lyre

Why didn't girls go to school?

Roman girls were expected to stay at home and learn how to run a household. This was training for when they were married. Most girls were taught how to play a musical instrument called the lyre.

What was a toga?

Toga

Most men wore a long robe called a toga.
It looked good, but it was bulky and uncomfortable to wear. Important men wore togas with a purple trim. Most children wore togas, too. Married ladies wore a dress called a 'stola' and a shawl called a 'palla' over the top of it.

Did people wear make-up?

Both men and women wore make-up. The Romans admired pale, smooth skin. Crushed chalk was used as face powder, red ochre (crumbly earth) for blusher and plant juice for lipstick.

Palla

Stola

'Scare' cut!
Going to the barbers could be very painful. Scissors and razors had not been invented. Barbers used big, sharp shears to trim men's hair and beards!

Hairstyles

Find out
What did Julius Caesar wear on his head?

What were Roman hairstyles like?

Hairstyles went in and out of fashion. Women would curl, plait or pin up their hair. Wigs and hair extensions were popular, as were headdresses and hairbands.

Who wore precious jewels?

Men and women wore rings of gold, silver or bronze. Many of these rings were decorated with amber or precious stones. Rich ladies wore necklaces and earrings of gold and pearls, while poorer women made do with beads of glass or ceramics. Cloaks were fastened with fine brooches.

Necklace

Ring

Earrings

Baby love!

Romans gave a good luck charm called a 'bulla' to their babies to keep them safe from harm.

What was a mosaic?

The Romans liked their homes to look good, too. Beautiful pictures called mosaics decorated floors. Each mosaic was made from thousands of small tiles made from coloured stone or pottery.

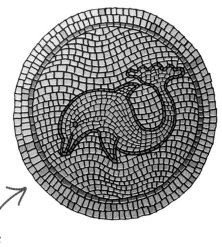

Mosaic

Make

Look at some Roman mosaics in a book then make your own using squares of coloured card.

Did people wear shoes?

Most people wore leather sandals. Soldiers wore these too, but with studded soles so they were not worn out by marching. Boots were worn for riding.

How clean were the Romans?

The Romans were very clean. They often visited the public baths. These huge buildings were also fitness centres and a place to meet friends. Visitors could take part in sports, such as wrestling, have a massage or even get their hair cut.

Cool bath

Cold bath

Fire to heat water

What a stink!

Although the Romans liked bathing, they only visited the baths once in every nine days.

Did the Romans listen to music?

The Romans liked music and dancing. Ordinary people liked listening to pipes, flutes, cymbals and horns. Rich people preferred the quieter sound of the lyre.

Roman bath house

Hot bath

Board game

What games did people play?

Popular Roman games were 'Tables', 'Robbers' and 'Three Stones' – a version of noughts-and-crosses. A favourite girls' game was tossing little bones into the air and seeing how many they could catch on the back of the hand.

What was the Colosseum?

The Colosseum was an amazing building. It was a huge oval arena in the centre of Rome, used for fights between men called gladiators, and for pretend sea battles. Up to 50,000 people could sit inside. It was built of stone, concrete and marble and had 80 entrances.

The Colosseum

Draw
Romans followed chariot racing like we support football. Draw a poster advertising a chariot race.

Did Romans race to the circus?

The Romans liked a day at the races. Horses pulled chariots around a track, called a 'circus'. The most famous was Circus Maximus. Twelve chariots took part in each race, running seven times round the track.

Superstars!

Some gladiators became so popular that people wrote graffiti about them on walls.

Chariot racing

Was chariot racing dangerous?

Yes it was. Chariots often smashed into each other and overturned. Each driver carried a sharp knife called a 'falx', to cut himself free if this happened. Many horses and drivers were killed.

What was army life like?

Roman soldiers were well paid and well cared for. They were often called upon to defend the Roman Empire from enemies, so the army was very important. Soldiers were trained in battle and often had to march long distances along straight roads.

Brrrr!

Roman soldiers guarding the cold northern frontiers of Britain kept warm by wearing short woollen trousers, like underpants, beneath their tunics!

Testudo

Was a tortoise used in battle?

When soldiers had to defend themselves against enemy attack, they used a 'tortoise'. Their shields made a protective 'shell' around them. It was called a 'testudo', or tortoise. Soldiers carried three main weapons – javelins, swords and daggers.

Did soldiers cook dinner?

Yes they did. Soldiers had to find or make everything they needed to survive. They built camps and forts defended by walls. Soldiers had to be able to cook, build, and be doctors, blacksmiths and engineers – and they all had to fight!

Roman soldiers

Discover

Can you find out which famous British queen the Romans had trouble defeating?

What was a villa?

Pets

Villas were large Roman country houses. They were surrounded by orchards, fields, flocks of sheep or herds of cattle. Country villas were owned mainly by the rich. The first villas were small farmhouses, but as Rome became powerful, villas became magnificent mansions.

Roman villa

Garden

Plan

Plan your own villa. Draw pictures of how it might look.

Did people keep pets?

Roman families liked to keep pets. Statues and paintings show many children playing with their pets. Dogs, cats and doves were all popular. Some families also kept ornamental fish and tame deer.

Love struck!

The Romans invented Valentine's Day, but called it 'Lupercalia'. Boys picked a girl's name from a hat, and she was meant to be their girlfriend for the year!

Bedroom

Kitchen

Where did people go on holiday?

In the summer, Rome became hot, stuffy, smelly and dirty. Rich Romans often had two homes, so they would leave the city and escape to their villa in the countryside.

Why were farms important?

In Roman times, most people lived and worked on farms. Without farms, the people of Rome would starve. Farmers produced food for city people, which was grown on big estates by teams of slaves, and on small peasant farms where single families worked together.

Squeaky clean!

When Romans bathed, they covered their bodies in olive oil and then scraped it off to remove all the dirt and sweat!

Farm

Olives

Why were olives so special?

Olives grow on trees. The Romans used them as food, or crushed them to make oil. Olive oil was used as medicine, in cooking, for cleansing the skin — and even for burning in lamps.

Imagine

Imagine you are a Roman farm worker, what job would you do and why?

Did grapes grow on trees?

Roman grapes did grow on trees, almost! Vines are climbing plants that produce grapes. The Romans planted them among fruit trees, which supported the vines as they grew.

Who was the top god?

The Romans worshipped many different gods. Jupiter was king of the gods. His wife Juno was worshipped by married women. Mars was the god of war and Venus was the goddess of love. Neptune, god of the sea, sent earthquakes and terrible storms. Messenger of the gods was Mercury.

Jupiter and Juno

Mars and Venus

Neptune

Find out

School children had their own goddess. Can you find out what she was called? Use a book to help you.

Did people go to church?

Temples were beautiful buildings. They were built so that people could worship the gods. At the centre was a shrine. Here, people would leave food and wine as gifts to the gods.

Temple

Which god started storms?

Neptune was god of the sea. The Romans believed he could start and stop storms. He was also the god of earthquakes. Sea travel was dangerous in Roman times, so sailors prayed to Neptune to keep them safe on their journeys.

Mercury

Why were roads always straight?

The Romans built thousands of kilometres of roads. They were built to link the rest of the empire to Rome itself. To make travel as fast as possible, roads were built in straight lines taking the shortest route.

Building a road

Look

The Romans invented concrete. Look outside – can you see anything made of concrete?

Could ships sail to Rome?

Most ships were too big to sail up the river Tiber to Rome. Instead, they stopped at Rome's main port, Ostia. Here, the ship's cargo was loaded onto smaller barges and taken the final 25 kilometres to Rome.

Roman ship

Crystal ball!

The Romans often consulted a fortune-teller or a priest even before setting out on a long journey.

Did people travel in their beds?

Town streets were crowded and very dirty. Rich people travelled in curtained beds called litters, carried shoulder-high by slaves. Ordinary people used stepping-stones to avoid the mud and rubbish on the streets.

Why was Rome so beautiful?

The Romans built beautiful buildings. They invented concrete, and used clay bricks baked at high temperatures, which lasted longer than unbaked ones. Arches were built to create strong walls and doorways. Huge domes were made for buildings that were too big for wooden roofs.

Pipe up!

Our word 'plumber' comes from 'plumbum', the Latin word for the lead used by Romans to make water pipes. The same word is also used for a 'plumb—line', still in use today.

Roman buildings

Were there doctors in Rome?

Yes there were, but the Romans believed that illness was caused by witchcraft. To find a cure, they visited a temple to ask the gods to make them better. They might see a doctor who made medicines from plants or carried out simple operations.

Doctor and patient

Find out

Romans spoke their own language. Can you find out what it was called?

How was Rome supplied with water?

Water from mountain springs was carried on raised stone channels into the city. Once the water reached the city, it flowed through pipes to baths, fountains and toilets.

Quiz time

Do you remember what you have read about ancient Rome? Here are some questions to test your memory. The pictures will help you. If you get stuck, read the pages again.

3. What did children learn at school?

page 376

4. What was a mosaic?

page 381

page 373

1. Did people live in blocks of flats?

page 382

5. How clean were the Romans?

page 375

6. Did the Romans listen to music?

page 383

2. Who ate takeaways?

page 384

7. What was the Colosseum?

11. Who was the top god?

page 392

8. Did people keep pets?

page 389

12. Did people travel in their beds?

page 395

13. Why was Rome so beautiful?

page 396

page 391

9. Why were olives so special?

Answers

1. Yes, Rome had the first high-rise flats
2. Poorer people
3. Writing, arithmetic, history, sport, public speaking
4. Pictures made from coloured stone or pottery
5. Very clean, they often visited the baths
6. Yes, they liked music and dancing
7. A huge oval arena used for gladiator fights and pretend sea battles
8. Yes they did
9. Because they were used as food and crushed to make oil that was used for many things
10. Grapes grew on vines that grew around trees
11. Jupiter
12. No, they travelled in litters
13. Because the Romans built beautiful buildings

10. Did grapes grow on trees?

page 391

Questions about...

Where did Vikings come from? 402
Who discovered Greenland? 403
Why did Vikings carry boats? 403

Which king killed his brother? 404
Who tried to stop the waves? 405
What was the Jelling Stone? 405

What was a dragon ship? 406
Did Vikings have maps? 406
Who was afraid of the Vikings? 407

Why were Vikings so fierce? 408
Did swords have names? 408
What weapons did Vikings use? 409

Who rode an eight-legged horse? 410
Who controlled the thunder? 411
Why were warriors so brave? 411

Why did animals live in houses? 412
What were runes? 413
Why did Vikings get ill? 413

How did grass provide food? 414
Did Vikings have factories? 415
Why was the sea so important? 415

What was sold at markets? 416
How were quarrels settled? 417
Who were the Vikings scared of? 417

Vikings

Did girls go to school?   418
Were wives expensive?   419
Who used wooden swords?   419

What did people wear?   420
Did people wear jewellery?   421
Did Vikings wear make up?   421

How did Vikings prepare
    for battle?   424
What was a saga?   425
What did people do for fun?   425

How did people get clean?   422
Did Vikings have toilets?   422
How did Vikings wear their hair? 423

Who defeated the Vikings?   426
How do we remember
    the Vikings?   427
Was Santa a Viking?   427

Quiz time   428

Where did Vikings come from?

The Vikings lived about 2000 years ago. Viking warriors came from Denmark, Sweden and Norway to raid villages and steal treasure. Viking families began to settle in England, Ireland, Scotland and France. They explored Iceland, Greenland and Russia — and even travelled as far as North America.

Viking warriors

Who discovered Greenland?

A Viking called Erik the Red discovered Greenland. It was a dark and icy place but Erik wanted people to come and live there. He called it 'Greenland' so they would think it was a warm place full of trees and grass.

Greenland

Imagine

Can you imagine discovering a new country? What would you call it?

Why did Vikings carry their boats?

In winter, Vikings made long overland journeys. In some places, they carried their boats over ground between rivers. The Vikings were brave adventurers, keen to seek new land and treasures. Each journey took several years.

Pirates!

The word 'Viking' means 'pirates', 'port-attackers', or 'people of the bays'. This tells us that Vikings spent their lives close to the sea.

Which king killed his brother?

When a Viking king died, each of his sons had an equal right to his throne. Erik Bloodaxe was famous for his cruelty. He wanted to be king so much, he killed both of his brothers and became King Erik of Norway.

Think

What would your Viking name be? You can make it as funny as you like!

Erik Bloodaxe

My name is...!

Many Viking rulers had strange names such as Svein Forkbeard, Einar Falsemouth, Magnus Barelegs, and Thorfinn Skullsplitter!

King Cnut

Who tried to stop the waves?

King Cnut was a Viking king of Denmark, Norway and England. He was a cruel ruler. However, Cnut said he was a good Christian. To prove it, he ordered the waves to stop. When they did not he said, "This proves that I am weak. Only God can control the sea."

What was the Jelling Stone?

King Harald Bluetooth built a church at Jelling, in Denmark. Outside the church was a memorial for his dead parents. It was called the Jelling Stone and was decorated with Viking and Christian carvings.

What was a dragon ship?

Vikings built ships called 'drakar', or dragon ships. These ships were designed for war. They were long, speedy and beautifully carved. Because they were so light, they could sail easily onto beaches.

Drakar ship

Did Vikings have maps?

No, they didn't. The Vikings used the positions of the Sun, Moon and stars to guide them on their travels. They also followed the direction the wind was blowing in.

Remember

Can you remember the Viking word for 'dragon ship'?

Gold to go away!

Viking pirates threatened to attack if they were not paid to sail away. This usually worked, and villages paid the gold — again and again!

Who was afraid of the Vikings?

Vikings could be very scary! People living in seaside villages were often afraid of them. Gangs of warriors carried out raids on defenceless villages. They stole valuable treasure and healthy young men and women to sell as slaves.

Viking raid

Why were Vikings so fierce?

To scare their enemies in battle! Viking warriors dressed in animal skins and charged at their enemies, howling and growling like wolves, and chewing at their shields. These warriors were called berserkirs and this is where the word 'berserk' comes from.

Berserkir

Did swords have names?

Viking warriors loved their swords so much, they even gave them names such as 'Sharp Biter'! When a warrior died, he would be buried with his sword by his side.

Shield

What weapons did Vikings use?

Vikings had to make or buy all of their weapons. Poor soldiers carried knives and spears. Wealthy Vikings had metal helmets and tunics, and fine, sharp swords. They carried a round shield that was made of wood covered with leather.

Sword

Helmet

Soldier women!

Women went to war but they did not fight. Instead, they nursed wounded warriors and cooked meals for hungry soldiers.

Who rode an eight-legged horse?

Odin

Odin was king of the Viking gods. He rode an eight-legged horse called Sleipnir and had two ravens called Thought and Memory. Odin sat on a high throne so he could see all of the Universe. Sometimes he liked to dress as a traveller and take a holiday in the human world.

Discover
Can you find out about any other Viking gods or goddesses – which one is your favourite?

Who controlled the thunder?

Thor

The storm god Thor controlled thunder. Viking farmers hated thunderstorms because they ruined their crops. They would pray to Thor to stop the thunder and let their crops grow. Thor rode in his chariot through the clouds holding a giant hammer and thunderbolt.

Sea god!

Njord was the god of the sea. He was married to the giantess Skadi, who watched over the mountains.

Why were warriors so brave?

Because they believed they would go to heaven when they died. Vikings thought that dead warriors were remembered forever, and that they went to heaven to feast with the gods.

Why did animals live in houses?

Homes were needed to shelter animals, as well as people. In towns, pigs, goats and horses were kept in sheds. In the countryside, the weather could be cold and wet. Farmers lived in longhouses, with an area for animals at one end. This meant that the people and animals stayed warm and dry.

Longhouse

Room for the animals

What were runes?

Runes were the 16 letters of the Viking alphabet. People used them for labelling belongings with the owner's name, recording accounts, keeping calendars and sending messages. There was no paper, so runes were carved onto wood.

← Runes

Make

With a cardboard box, make your own Viking house. You could even glue some grass to the roof.

Why did Vikings get ill?

Vikings suffered from chest diseases. This was because their houses did not have windows and were often damp and full of smoke from the fire burning on the stove.

Grass roof

Outside toilet

Precious cow!

Viking farmers loved cows! A cow was precious because it gave milk, clothing and meat, and its droppings were spread on the fields to help crops grow.

How did grass provide food?

Grassy fields provided food for animals and people. Sheep and cows needed fresh grass to eat. These animals then provided milk and meat for people to eat. Farmers also cut the grass and dried it out to make hay to feed the animals in the winter.

Farm

Discover
Have a look at the labels inside your clothes. What are your clothes made of?

Did Vikings have factories?

No! Vikings had no machines, so all work was done by hand. Families had to make or grow everything they needed. They built their own houses and furniture and they made their own clothes and toys. Blacksmiths made weapons and tools for people to work with.

Blacksmiths

Why was the sea so important?

Because people could catch fish to eat. People also gathered shellfish from the seashore for dinner. Vikings built their villages close to the sea in case they needed to travel to new places.

Itchy clothes!

Clothes were made of wool and could be very itchy. Women made smoother, finer cloth to wear as underwear.

What was sold at markets?

Vikings held markets on the beach. Farmers would sell meat, milk and fur to travellers. Some Vikings travelled a long way to buy different things to sell. They would buy woollen cloth from Britain, wine from France, glass from Germany, jewellery from Russia and spices from the Middle East.

Market

How were quarrels settled?

Many quarrels were settled by fighting. Quarrels between families could continue for months. This lead to people on both sides being killed, until each family was prepared to seek peace.

Settling an argument

Bone comb!

Animal bones that were left over from mealtimes were used to carve combs, beads and pins. Deer antlers were used to make finer combs.

Pretend

With a friend, pretend to be a pirate and Viking. Who is more scared of who?

Who were the Vikings scared of?

Pirates from Russia! They sailed across the sea to steal treasure from Viking towns. So Vikings defended their towns with wooden walls and troops of warriors.

Did girls go to school?

No, they didn't. Instead of going to school, girls helped their mothers with cooking and cleaning, fed farm animals, fetched water, gathered wood, nuts and berries and learned how to spin, weave and sew.

Viking girls

Think
Can you think why it was important for young boys to practise fighting with wooden swords?

Were wives expensive?

If a Viking man wanted to marry, he had to ask the woman's father for permission and pay him a bride price. If the father accepted this, the marriage went ahead, even if the woman did not agree.

Who used wooden swords?

Viking boys practised fighting with wooden swords and small, lightweight shields. They also learned how to ride horses and use real weapons. They had to be ready to fight by the time they were 15 or 16 years old.

Viking boys

Wise women!

Many young women died having a baby. This meant there were fewer older women. Older women were thought to be very wise and people respected them for their knowledge and experience.

What did people wear?

Vikings wore lots of layers to keep out the cold. Women wore long dresses of linen or wool with a woollen over-dress. Men dressed in wool tunics over linen shirts and woollen trousers. Men also wore fur or sheepskin caps while women wore headscarves and shawls.

Dress up

Have a look through your wardrobe and see if you can dress up as a Viking!

Clothing

Did people wear jewellery?

Both men and women liked to wear lots of jewellery. They thought it made them look good and it also showed how rich they were. Rings and arm braclets were given to warriors as rewards for fighting bravely in battle.

Gold ring

Necklace

Brooch

Did Vikings wear make up?

Viking men wore make-up! They particularly liked to wear make up around their eyes – probably made from soot or crushed berries. They thought it made them look more handsome.

How did people get clean?

Vikings bathed by pouring water over red-hot stones to create clouds of steam. They sat in the steam to make themselves sweat, then rubbed their skin with birch twigs to help loosen the dirt. Then they jumped into a pool of cold water to rinse off.

Keeping clean

Did Vikings have toilets?

Yes they did. Houses had an outside toilet that was simply a bucket, or a hole in the ground with a wooden seat on top. Panels of woven twigs were set up around the toilet. Dried moss or grass was used as toilet paper.

Hairstyles

How did Vikings wear their hair?

Men let their fringes grow long, and plaited the strands that hung down either side of their face. Women also kept their hair long. They left it flowing loose until they married, then tied it in a beautiful knot at the nape of their neck.

How did Vikings prepare for battle?

Viking sports were good training for war. Spear-throwing, sword-fighting and archery – shooting at targets with bows and arrows – were all popular. They helped boys and young men to become fit and strong and prepared them for using weapons.

Archer →

Drinking horns

Vikings liked to drink ale from cups carved from cattle horns. Warriors would carry these drinking horns on their long journeys.

What was a saga?

A saga was a story that Vikings told to honour heroes who died in battle. The sagas were told to ensure that heroes' names and fame never died. These stories were passed on by word of mouth for many years.

Saga

What did people do for fun?

Vikings liked music and dancing. Kings would hire dancers, clowns, jugglers and singers to entertain their guests at feasts. Vikings also enjoyed playing practical jokes and listening to stories about gods and heroes.

Write

What is your favourite story? Maybe you could try and write one of your own.

Who defeated the Vikings?

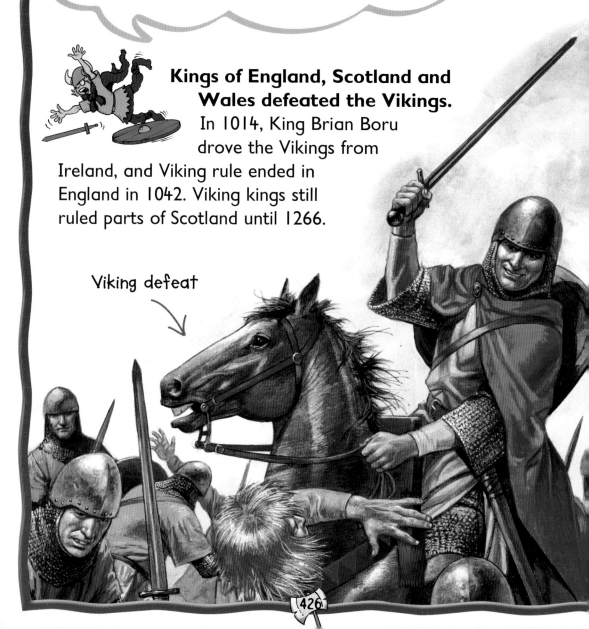

Kings of England, Scotland and Wales defeated the Vikings. In 1014, King Brian Boru drove the Vikings from Ireland, and Viking rule ended in England in 1042. Viking kings still ruled parts of Scotland until 1266.

Viking defeat

426

Find out

Try to find any other Viking words that we still use today. Ask an adult to help you.

Festival

How do we remember the Vikings?

Today, people still celebrate Viking festivals. In the Shetland Isles, people dress up as Vikings then burn a lifesize model of a Viking warship. They do this to remember the Viking festival of Yule, held every January.

Was Santa a Viking?

Santa was a Viking god! Yule (mid-winter) was an important Viking festival. Vikings held feasts and exchanged gifts. They also believed that Viking gods travelled across the sky, bringing good things – just like Santa!

Do you speak Viking?

Many Viking words for everyday things still survive such as 'sister', 'knife' and 'egg'.

Quiz time

Do you remember what you have read about the Vikings? These questions will test your memory. The pictures will help you. If you get stuck, read the pages again.

page 403

1. Why did Vikings carry their boats?

2. Which king killed his brother?

page 404

3. Who was afraid of the Vikings?

page 407

4. Did swords have names?

page 408

5. Who controlled the thunder?

page 411

6. Why did animals live in houses?

page 412

7. Why was the sea so important?

page 415

page 422

11. Did Vikings have toilets?

8. Who used wooden swords?

page 419

12. Who defeated the Vikings?

page 426

9. Were wives expensive?

page 419

page 427

13. Was Santa a Viking?

10. How did people get clean?

page 422

Answers

1. To transport them between rivers
2. Erik Bloodaxe
3. People living in seaside villages
4. Viking warriors gave their swords names
5. Thor, the storm god
6. To keep them warm and dry
7. So people could catch fish to eat
8. Viking boys
9. Viking men had to pay money to their bride's father
10. They steamed themselves
11. Yes, they did
12. Kings of England, Scotland and Wales
13. Yes, Santa was a Viking god

Questions
about...

Why were castles built on hills?   432
Were all castles made from wood?   433
What was a moat?   433

What was inside the castle?   434
Where was the safest place?   435
How did people get bread
    and water?   435

What happened at knight school?   436
Who had the best horses?   437
What was dubbing?   437

Knights & Castles

Did knights fight with a ball? 438
Did knights wear woolly jumpers? 439
How long was the Hundred
   Years War? 439

Did knights have fun? 442
Did knights only fight on
   horseback? 442
How did knights find a wife? 443

How were knights told apart? 440
What was a herald? 441
Where did soldiers meet? 441

What was a siege? 444
How did the castle crumble? 445
How did enemies get inside
   a castle? 445

Quiz time 446

Why were castles built on hills?

People began building castles over 1000 years ago. They were built on a hill so that people could see the enemy better. The hill was made from a huge mound of mud and stones. It was called a motte.

Motte

Were all castles made from wood?

Early castles were made from wood. They were not very strong and they caught fire easily. People began to build stone castles. These were much stronger. They lasted longer and did not burn.

Stone castle

Slimy walls!

Builders often covered wooden castles with wet, slippery leather. This stopped them from burning so easily.

What was a moat?

Builders dug a big ditch around the castle. Then they filled it with water. This watery ditch was called a moat. Enemy soldiers got wet and cold if they attacked the castle from the moat. It was hard to fight from the bottom of it, too!

Think

Stone castles were a lot warmer in winter than wooden ones. Why do you think this was so?

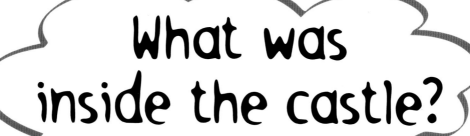

What was inside the castle?

A big courtyard was inside the castle. This was called a bailey. A thick wall was built all around it. Smaller buildings were put up inside the bailey. Sometimes there were gardens. There were often animals and chickens, too!

Thick wall

Where was the safest place?

The safest place in the castle was a tall, strong tower. This tower was called a keep. The lord of the castle lived there with his family. In later times they slept on the top floor. There were big rooms downstairs to hold feasts for visitors.

Keep

Thick walls!

The walls of the keep were at least 3.5 metres thick! This meant that building a castle took a long time. It was also a very expensive job.

Water wheel

How did people get bread and water?

A castle often had its own mill and bakery. Many castles got water from a well. The well was dug inside the bailey. A massive wheel drew water up into the castle. Later castles had piped water with taps.

Measure

The keep walls were 3.5 metres thick. Use a tape measure to see how thick this is.

What happened at knight school?

A knight had to train for 14 years! First, he went to a lord's house when he was seven years old. There, he was taught how to ride and to shoot with a bow. Then he became a squire and was taught how to fight with a sword.

Teacher

Count

A nobleman's son went to knight school when he was seven. He studied for 14 years. How old was he when he became a knight?

Who had the best horses?

Rich knights owned three horses. The heaviest horse was used for fighting and in tournaments. The quickest was used for long journeys. The third carried the bags!

Knight and his horse

Dying for love!

Jaufre Rudel was a French knight. He sent love letters to the beautiful Countess of Tripoli, even though had never seen her! When he finally met her he fell into her arms and died!

Squire

What was dubbing?

A new knight was given a special ceremony called a dubbing. First, he had to spend a whole night in church, praying on his knees. Then the new knight was tapped on the shoulder with a sword.

Did knights fight with a ball?

Morning star

Knights hit the enemy with a spiked ball on a long chain. This was called a 'morning star.'

Knights used swords, too. Foot knights from Switzerland used a halberd. This was an axe with a hook on the back. It was good for getting a knight off his horse!

Sword

Get to the point!

Soldiers called 'retrievers' fetched all the fallen arrows. They had to run through the battle to get them!

Knight dressed for battle

Chainmail

Tunic

Did knights wear woolly jumpers?

A knight in early times wore a bright tunic with long sleeves. It was made from wool or linen. He also wore metal armour called chainmail. It looked and felt like knitted wire! A padded jacket stopped the chainmail from scratching the skin.

Design

In later times, knights wore steel armour. They even wore metal shoes! Design your own suit of armour to protect a knight.

How long was the Hundred Years War?

The Hundred Years War was fought between the English and the French. It actually lasted for 116 years, between 1337 and 1453. English and Welsh soldiers used longbows against the French. The bowmen could fire 12 arrows every minute!

How were knights told apart?

A knight wore a helmet that covered his head. Even his soldiers could not recognize him! Each knight put a special symbol on his shield and robes. The symbols and colours were called a 'coat of arms'.

Don't shoot the messenger!

Using a coat of arms was called 'heraldry'. This is because the lord's messenger was called a 'herald'. The herald wore his lord's coat of arms as he crossed the battlefield.

Knight wearing coat of arms

What was a herald?

A herald was a messenger. He carried messages for knights during battles. The herald had to be able recognize each knight by his coat of arms. The heralds were very good at recognizing coats of arms. This eventually came to be known as heraldry.

Herald

Horse wearing coat of arms

Where did soldiers meet?

Each lord had a banner with his coat of arms on it. Knights and soldiers gathered around the banner on the battlefield. The lord could then explain his battle plans. The winner of a battle often stole the enemy's banner from him.

Make

Draw and cut out a shield from cardboard. Paint your own symbol on it.

Did knights have fun?

Yes they did! Knights took part in competitions called tournaments. These helped them to improve their fighting. The knights formed two teams that fought each other in pretend battles.

Did knights only fight on horseback?

At a tournament, knights also fought on the ground. They wore heavy armour. Skill and speed were much more important than strength.

Make

Write and design a programme for a tournament. You can include fighting competitions and entertainment.

Rotten cheat!

Some knights tried to cheat in a jousting competition. They wore special armour that was fixed to the horse's saddle!

Knight taking part in a tournament

Jousting knight

How did knights find a wife?

Ladies from the king's court went to tournaments. The knights showed off their bravery to their favourite lady. Each knight tried to push another knight off his horse with a long pole called a lance. This was called jousting.

What was a siege?

People sometimes became trapped inside a castle if the enemy surrounded it. This was called a siege. The people inside could not get food supplies. So they had a terrible choice. They could either starve to death or surrender to the enemy.

Castle under attack

Think
Try to think of ways to get into a castle without being seen. Look at the castle on page 18 to help you find a way in. Draw a map of your route.

How did the castle crumble?

Sometimes the enemy bashed down the castle gates with battering rams. These were thick tree trunks capped with iron. The enemy also tried to climb the walls with giant ladders. Huge catapults hurled burning wood and stones.

Battering ram

Siege

Hairy weapons!

Giant catapults were wound up with ropes made of human hair! The hair was made into plaits and was very strong.

How did enemies get inside a castle?

Sometimes enemy soldiers dug tunnels underneath the castle. They then popped up inside the castle walls. The enemy also pushed wooden towers against the castle walls. Soldiers hiding in the towers leapt out and climbed into the castle.

Quiz time

Do you remember what you have read about knights and castles? These questions will test your memory. The pictures will help you. If you get stuck, read the pages again.

3. Where was the safest place?

page 435

4. What happened at knight school?

page 436

1. Why were castles built on hills?

page 432

5. What was dubbing?

page 437

2. What was a moat?

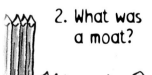

page 433

6. Did knights fight with a ball?

page 438

7. Did knights wear woolly jumpers?

page 439

8. How were knights told apart?

page 440

9. Where did soldiers meet?

page 441

10. Did knights only fight on horseback?

page 443

11. How did a knight find a wife?

page 443

12. How did the castle crumble?

page 445

13. How did enemies get inside a castle?

page 445

Answers

1. So people could see the enemy
2. A watery ditch around a castle
3. The keep
4. Boys were trained to be knights
5. A special ceremony for a new knight
6. They fought with a spiked ball on a chain
7. No, they wore chainmail and tunics
8. By coats of arms
9. Around the banner on the battlefield
10. No, they also fought on the ground
11. When he was jousting
12. The walls were bashed with battering rams
13. They dug tunnels under the castle

Questions about...

What is a pirate?   450
Who was afraid of the
    Barbarossas?   451
Did all pirates want treasure?   451

Who stole the Spanish gold?   452
When were pirates not pirates?   453
Can you be a pirate with
    one leg?   453

Could women be pirates?   456
Whose prisoners ate caterpillars?   457
Who said she was sorry?   457

What were the best ships?   458
Where did pirates sleep?   458
What did pirates eat?   459

Did sailors fight the pirates?   454
What did pirates do with
    their money?   454
Where was there a pirate
    paradise?   455

Who was afraid of a flag?   460
Were buccaneers heroes?   460
Where was the treasure?   461

Pirates

What were pirates scared of? 464
How did pirates find their way? 465
How did pirates save
   a sinking ship? 465

Who is Long John Silver? 466
What ate Captain Hook's hand? 467
Did pirates sing? 467

Quiz time 468

What was the best treasure? 462
Was the treasure shared? 463
Where were all the jewels? 463

What is a pirate?

A pirate attack

Pirates are people who steal from ships and ports. As soon as the first ships began to carry goods, pirates began to attack them. About 600 years ago, there were many pirates sailing on the seas and oceans around the world.

Hairy pirates!

'Barbarossa' was a nickname for two pirate brothers. 'Barbarossa' means 'Redbeard' — because they both had red beards!

Who was afraid of the Barbarossas?

Every sailor was afraid of the two Barbarossa brothers! They were pirates who attacked ships about 500 years ago. One of the brothers captured the town of Algiers in North Africa. The other attacked ships that belonged to the Pope, who was the leader of the Christian church.

Make

Make your own Barbarossa mask. Draw your pirate's face on card. Use red wool to make a big red beard.

Did all pirates want treasure?

Pirates from the Mediterranean were called corsairs. They didn't want treasure. Instead, they took people from ships and ports and sold them as slaves. Corsairs also captured rich people. They were paid a lot of money to release them.

Corsairs and their ships

Who stole the Spanish gold?

About 500 years ago, Spanish captains sailed to the Americas. There they found gold, silver and jewels. The Spanish stole it from the American people and took it back to Spain. Pirates often attacked the Spanish ships before they got home and took the treasure from them.

Spanish captains and their treasure

When were pirates not pirates?

Act

Try to act out your own story about Spanish and English captains. One is trying to steal treasure from the other.

English captains such as John Hawkins raided Spanish treasure ships. England and Spain were enemies at this time, so the English thought it was okay to steal from the Spanish. The captains wanted to be called 'privateers' instead of 'pirates'.

Pirate queen!

Queen Elizabeth I of England encouraged her sea captains to be privateers. However, the privateers were often robbed before they reached England!

Can you be a pirate with one leg?

Francois Le Clerc

Yes! Francois Le Clerc was a dangerous pirate with just one leg. In the 1550s, he raided Caribbean islands owned by Spain. He captured the port of Havana on the island of Cuba. No one would pay Le Clerc to give up the port, so he burned it to the ground.

Did sailors fight the pirates?

Sailors fought hard against pirates when they were attacked. But they didn't try to fight Francis L'Ollonais in the 1660s. He was very cruel and tortured his prisoners. When Francis attacked a ship, the captain and sailors usually gave up without a fight.

Captain surrendering

What did pirates do with their money?

Pirates sold their treasure to people at the docks. They usually made lots of money. Most of the money was spent in public houses!

Spend! Spend! Spend!

Pirates could spent 3000 pieces of silver in one night. That's about ₤45,000 in today's money!

Francis L'Ollonais

Where was there a pirate paradise?

Port Royal was a harbour on the island of Jamaica. A strong fort guarded the harbour. Pirates could even mend their ships in the docks. Jamaica was ruled by the English, who left the pirates alone.

Paint

Paint a pirate scene with ships and a port. There might be lots of ships, with the pirates carrying their treasure onto dry land.

Pirates in Port Royal

Could women be pirates?

Yes, they could! Mary Read dressed up as a man and became a sailor in the 1700s. Her ship was raided by pirates and Mary decided to join them. Her ship was raided by 'Calico Jack' and his wife, Anne Bonney. Mary made friends with Anne and they fought against the navy.

Mary Read and Anne Bonney

Make

Make a plate of food for a pirate's prisoner! Take a paper plate and stick on cut-out food – such as caterpillars!

Whose prisoners ate caterpillars?

Ching Shih was a Chinese pirate. In 1807, she controlled many ships that raided China's coast. Ching Shih was a great leader. She had very strict rules for her sailors. Her prisoners had to eat caterpillars in boiled rice!

Ching Shih

Baldy!

Grace O'Malley shaved her head to look more like her sailors. She was given the nickname 'Baldy'!

Who said she was sorry?

Grace O'Malley went to sea when she was a young girl. She ended up controlling pirate ships off the coast of Ireland. Grace had 20 ships under her command. In 1593 Grace asked Queen Elizabeth I of England to forgive her for being a pirate.

What were the best ships?

A galley ship

Pirate ships had to be very fast! Many were small and easy to sail. Schooners were ships that had two masts. Corsairs sailed in galleys – ships that had oars as well as sails. The captain had a cabin in the stern (back of the ship). Treasure, gunpowder and food were stored in the hold, beneath the deck.

Stern (back)

Oars

Water and stores (middle)

Where did pirates sleep?

Most pirates slept on the deck unless the weather was bad. Some put up hammocks below deck in the middle of the ship. It was cramped, smelly and noisy. This made some pirates ill. So did their food. They didn't eat enough fruit and vegetables!

Recycling!

Pirates even stole their prisoners' clothes! They usually sold them, but sometimes kept the best items for themselves.

Sails

Write

Look at the picture of the galley. Write a guided tour of the ship. Describe how the pirates lived on it, too.

Bow (front)

What did pirates eat?

Pirates mostly ate dry biscuits and pickled meat when on board ship. They hunted for fresh meat when they landed on islands. They also collected fresh water and fruit. Pirate cooks often had only one arm or leg. They couldn't fight, so they cooked!

Who was afraid of a flag?

Merchant seamen were terrified when they saw the flag of a pirate ship. Early flags were bright red. By the 1700s, pirates flew black flags. Each pirate captain added his or her own symbol. Sometimes this was the famous white skull-and-crossbones.

Were buccaneers heroes?

Buccaneers were violent thieves. Some people thought they were heroes. Bartholomew Roberts was a buccaneer. His nickname was Black Bart. He was handsome and bold, yet he never drank anything stronger than tea! In the 1720s, he captured 400 ships.

Pirate flag

Duck!

When pirates attacked a ship, they shot at sailors working on the sails. They also shot at the helm, the steering area of the ship.

Where was the treasure?

Sailors often hid their treasure. Pirates had to break down walls and doors to find it. They threatened their prisoners until they revealed the treasure. Pirates had frightening weapons such as knives, daggers and pistols.

Design

Design your own pirate flag. Choose a bold colour. You could draw your own frightening symbol on it.

Pirates looking for treasure

What was the best treasure?

Gold and silver was the best pirate treasure. It could be gold or silver coins, plain bars or made into fine ornaments. Silk cloth and hardwoods such as ebony were also valuable. So was ivory. But pirates were not so happy with cotton, coal or iron.

Pirates and their stolen treasure

Spicy sands!

Spices from India and Sri Lanka were very valuable, but they were difficult to sell. Pirates often dumped them overboard. These spices piled up on the beaches.

Was the treasure shared?

The captain was in charge of sharing out the treasure. Officers got more than ordinary sailors. The cook and the carpenter got less because they didn't fight. Captains tried to divide everything fairly. Unhappy pirates might attack the captain and take over the ship!

Make

Make a mini treasure chest. Take a small box and paint it to look like wood. Then fill it with painted cut-out jewels.

Where were all the jewels?

Pirates stole jewels from ships all over the world. Diamonds came from Africa. Red rubies and blue sapphires came from Burma. Green emeralds were mined in Colombia. Divers scooped up shiny pearls from the Persian Gulf.

Treasure chest

What were pirates scared of?

Shipwreck was a pirate's greatest fear. Terrible storms could blow up in the warm waters around the Caribbean, the Indian Ocean and the Far East. In 1712, a storm blasted Port Royal in Jamaica. Winds smashed ships to pieces.

Shipwreck

Telescope

Compass

Map

How did pirates find their way?

Pirates used the position of the Sun and stars to guide them in the right direction. They also used a compass to help them. A telescope helped pirates to see landmarks and work out their position. Pirates used maps to find their way on land.

Write

Pretend you are captain of a pirate ship. Write down all the jobs that are carried out on board every day.

Round and round!

Captain William Dampier was a brilliant navigator. This means he knew where he was going! In the 1680s he sailed around the world three times.

How did pirates save a sinking ship?

Pirates tried to pump out water if the ship was leaking. Sometimes ships 'ran aground'. This means they got stuck in shallow water. The pirates had to throw out anything heavy. This helped the ship to refloat. Sometimes they threw out food barrels and cannons.

Who is Long John Silver?

Long John Silver is a one-legged pirate. But he isn't real! He appears in a book called *Treasure Island*. This adventure story is all about pirates and buried treasure. It was written by Robert Louis Stevenson in 1883.

Long John Silver

Dancing pirates!

Blackbeard was a real and dangerous pirate. In 1798, his story was made into a ballet!

What ate Captain Hook's hand?

Captain Hook is a fierce pirate in a story called *Peter Pan*. It was written as a book and a play by J.M. Barrie in 1904. Peter Pan is the hero. He cut off Captain Hook's hand and fed it to a crocodile. That's why the Captain needed a hook.

Captain Hook

Did pirates sing?

Gilbert and Sullivan were famous songwriters. They wrote a musical about pirates in 1879, called *Pirates of Penzance*. But the pirates were softies! They wouldn't steal from orphans — children who had no parents — so everyone pretended to be an orphan!

Write

Write your own pirate story. Your pirates can be kind or cruel. They could be modern pirates. What would treasure be like today?

Quiz time

Do you remember what you have read about pirates? These questions will test your memory. The pictures will help you. If you get stuck, read the pages again.

1. What is a pirate?

page 450

2. Who was afraid of the Barbarossas?

page 451

3. When were pirates not pirates?

page 453

4. Did sailors fight the pirates?

page 454

5. What did pirates do with their money?

page 454

6. Could women be pirates?

page 456

7. Whose prisoners ate caterpillars?

page 457

8. Where did pirates sleep?

page 458

9. What did pirates eat?

page 459

page 460

10. Who was afraid of a flag?

11. Where were all the jewels?

page 463

12. How did pirates find their way?

page 465

13. What ate Captain Hook's hand?

page 467

Answers

1. A person who steals from ships and ports
2. All sailors
3. When they were privateers
4. Yes, sailors fought hard against pirates
5. They spent it in public houses
6. Yes, they could
7. Ching Shih's prisoners
8. On the deck, or below deck in hammocks
9. Dry biscuits and pickled meat
10. Merchant seamen
11. Jewels came from all over the world
12. With a compass, telescope and map
13. A crocodile

Questions about...

Who wanted to find a
  magical land?   472
Who crossed the Alps with
  elephants?   473
Who were the best sailors?   473

Who was Marco Polo?   474
What did Marco Polo discover?   475
Who searched for a gold city?   475

Which explorer was very unlucky?   476
Why did explorers travel in junk? 477
Who was not allowed to explore?   477

Who brought back a giraffe?   478
Who found the route to Asia?   479
Why were spices like gold?   479

Who found the Americas?   480
Why did Columbus make
  a mistake?   481
Where was Vinland?   481

Who played a nasty trick?   482
Why did a dog get paid?   483
How did explorers tell the time?   483

Which city was hiding?   484
Who founded the New World?   485
Who tried to sail around
  the world?   485

Explorers

Who went on an important
   mission?   486
What was scurvy?   486
Which explorer went missing?   487

Who first crossed America?   488
Who went exploring in disguise?   489
Who was scared by bears?   489

Who tried to get to the
   North Pole?   490
Who crossed Australia?   491
Who were the first Australians?   491

Did explorers travel by sled?   492
Who conquered Everest?   493
How did explorers keep warm at
   the North Pole?   493

Who explored the natural world?   494
Who discovered nine cities?   494
Which ship explored the seabed?   495

How did people get to the Moon?   496
Who was the first man
   on the Moon?   497
Who was the first human
   in space?   497

Quiz time   498

Who wanted to find a magical land?

 In ancient times, Egyptian queen Hatshepsut sent explorers to look for a magical land. The land, called Punt, was full of treasure and beautiful animals. Hatshepsut's sailors brought back gold, ivory, monkeys and perfumes for the queen.

Flat world!

The ancient Egyptians thought the world was flat and rectangular, with the sea running around the edge.

Queen Hatshepsut

Who crossed the Alps with elephants?

In 22 BC Hannibal Barca, a famous military leader, invaded Italy. To get to Rome, and avoid being attacked, he took 46,000 soldiers and 37 war elephants across the Alps. It was one of the greatest military operations ever carried out in ancient times.

Hannibal

Who were the best sailors?

The best sailors in ancient times were the Phoenicians (say 'fuh-nee-shuns'). They came from what is now Syria and Lebanon and sailed all over the Mediterranean Sea. The Phoenicians used ships that had sails and oars.

Who was Marco Polo?

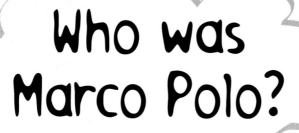

Marco Polo was a famous explorer who lived in Italy in the 1200s. He travelled to Asia at a time when most people in Europe never went far from their homes. Altogether, Marco travelled over 40,000 kilometres.

Marco Polo →

Think

Imagine that you are a famous explorer. Write a list of everything you would need to take on your travels.

What did Marco Polo discover?

Marco Polo discovered lots of amazing inventions on his travels through Asia. He saw fireworks, paper money, ice-cream and eyeglasses for the first time. He also discovered that the Chinese had a postage system and could post each other letters.

Empty deserts!

On the way to China, Marco Polo crossed the vast, empty Desert of Lop, now called the Gobi Desert.

Who searched for a gold city?

In the 1500s, Spanish explorers searched for a mysterious city called El Dorado. Everything in the city was said to be made of gold. However, they never found the city, and people believed that the gold had been melted down and sent abroad.

Which explorer was very unlucky?

In the 1300s, Moroccan explorer Ibn Battuta, dreamt that a giant bird picked him up and carried him away. Battuta thought that the dream was a sign from God, telling him to go exploring. During his travels he did not have much luck. He was kept prisoner, chased by pirates, attacked by thieves and shipwrecked.

Ibn Battuta

Why did explorers travel in junk?

A junk was a giant Chinese sailing ship. In ancient times, Zheng He, a Chinese explorer, had the largest sailing junks on Earth. The biggest was 130 metres long and 60 metres wide.

Discover

Where did you last go on holiday? How did you get there? How long did it take you?

Who was not allowed to explore?

Xuan-Zang, an ancient explorer, was banned from exploring by the Chinese emperor. He sneaked out of China and returned 16 years later with holy books and statues. The emperor was so pleased, he gave him a royal welcome.

Family values!

In many of the places Ibn Battuta visited, he got married. He had several wives and children in different parts of the world!

Who brought back a giraffe?

The Chinese sailor, Zheng He Zheng, was one of the world's best explorers. In the 1400s, he sailed to Africa. On his travels he collected precious stones, plants and animals to take back to the emperor. The emperor's favourite present was a giraffe from east Africa.

Zheng He Zheng

Star sailing!

Before the compass was invented, the first explorers had to rely on their observations of the Moon and stars to find their way.

Discover

Can you name any spices? Do you know any foods that have spices in them?

Vasco da Gama

Who found the route to Asia?

In the 1400s, Portugese sailor Vasco da Gama sailed to Calicut in India to find spices. The rajah, Calicut's ruler, did not let da Gama take any spices, so he went home empty-handed. However, the King of Portugal was very happy that da Gama had found the sea route to Asia.

Why were spices like gold?

In the 1400s, spices such as cinnamon and nutmeg were as valuable as gold. Spices came from Asia and were carried to Europe on the backs of camels. This took a long time and made them very expensive to buy.

Who found the Americas?

Christopher Columbus found the Americas by mistake! He wanted to sail around the world to Asia in his ship the *Santa Maria*. When Columbus spotted land in 1492, he thought he had sailed to Japan. In fact, he had found the Bahamas, just off the American mainland.

Santa Maria →

Discover
Which sea is closest to where you live? Look in an atlas or on a map to find out.

Why did Columbus make a mistake?

Because he had travelled to the wrong place! As Columbus thought he had arrived in Asia, he called the lands he found the West Indies, and the people he met, Indians. They are still called this today – even though the West Indies are thousands of miles from India.

Christopher Columbus

Hot stuff!

Sailors were afraid to sail around Africa. This was because of a myth that said if people went too far south in the Atlantic Ocean, the Sun would burn them to ashes.

Where was Vinland?

Five hundred years before Columbus, the Vikings found a new land and called it Vinland. They left after they kept getting into fights with the local people. Today, Vinland is known as America.

Who played a nasty trick?

The Spanish explorer Francisco Pizarro captured the Inca leader Atahuallpa in 1532. Atahuallpa said that if Pizarro set him free, he would give him a room filled with gold. Pizarro agreed. Once Atahuallpa had handed over the gold, Pizarro killed him and took over the Inca capital city, Cuzco.

Francisco Pizarro

Why did a dog get paid?

Spanish explorer Vasco Nuñez de Balboa sailed to America in 1500 looking for treasure. He took his beloved dog, Leoncico, with him. Leoncico never left his master's side and Balboa even paid him his own wage.

Whale of a time!

When sailing past Scotland, Greek explorer Pytheas was amazed to see fish as big as boats. In fact they weren't fish — they were whales.

Vasco Nuñez de Balboa

How did explorers tell the time?

Explorers could not tell the time at sea because clocks didn't work on ships. John Harrison, an inventor, created a new clock (called the chronometer) that could measure the time precisely, even at sea.

Look

Next time you go on a journey, write down how many different kinds of animals you see.

Which city was hiding?

 In the 1400s, the Inca people of South America built a city called Machu Picchu on top of a mountain. Built from large stones and watered by a spring at the top of the mountain, the city was so well-hidden, that Spanish invaders never found it. An American explorer re-discovered the city in 1911.

Machu Picchu

Play

With your friends, play a game of hide and seek. Take it in turns to be the hider and the seeker.

Who founded the New World?

In 1607, 100 British people arrived in what is now called the United States of America. They founded the first permanent settlement and others soon followed. The continent was named the New World, and Europe, Asia and Africa became known as the Old World.

Ferdinand Magellan

Rich pickings!

In the 1500s, Francis Drake captured a Spanish treasure ship. It was carrying a cargo that was worth more than £12 million in today's money.

Who tried to sail around the world?

Portuguese explorer, Ferdinand Magellan, wanted to sail around the world during the 1500s. Magellan thought he could get to Asia and buy spices. Many of his crew died from a disease called scurvy and Magellan himself was killed in war. Only one of his five ships sailed home safely.

Who went on an important mission?

In 1768, Captain James Cook was sent on an important mission by the British navy. He went to the island of Tahiti and made observations of the planet Venus passing in front of the Sun. He also explored Australia, New Zealand and the Pacific Islands and made new maps.

What was scurvy?

Scurvy is a serious disease that is caused by not eating enough fresh fruit and vegetables. Many explorers and sailors suffered from the disease when on long voyages, as they had no access to fruit and vegetables.

Dr Livingstone

Captain Cook

Which explorer went missing?

In 1869, the explorer Dr Livingstone went missing. He'd gone exploring in east Africa and no one had heard from him. Everyone thought he had died. An American writer, Henry Stanley, found him in Tanzania. He greeted him with the words, "Dr Livingstone, I presume?"

Tasty trip!

Captain Cook was the first European to discover Hawaii, in 1778. He called it the Sandwich Island.

Who first crossed America?

Meriwether Lewis and William Clark travelled across America in 1803.

They sailed down rivers on a boat. When the rivers grew too narrow, Lewis and Clark used canoes. Local Native American guides helped them paddle their canoe and find their way across America.

Lewis and Clark

Brotherly love!

Lewis and Clark met some fierce native warriors whilst exploring. By amazing chance, the warrior leader turned out to be the brother of their guide.

Who went exploring in disguise?

The French explorer Rene Caillie wanted to visit the ancient city of Timbuktu, but only Muslims were allowed in. He dressed up as an Arab trader and sneaked into the city in 1828. He was the first European to go there and return home alive.

Rene Caillie

Make it

Create a disguise for yourself using hats, sunglasses and old clothes. Does anyone recognize you?

Who was scared by bears?

American explorer Meriwether Lewis was chased by a bear whilst out hunting. Lewis tried to shoot the bear, but he ran out of bullets. The bear chased Lewis into a river, then walked away and left him alone.

Who tried to get to the North Pole?

 Norwegian explorer, Fridtjof Nansen did. He built a ship called *Fram*, which was designed to get stuck in the ice without being damaged. It was the strongest wooden ship of its time. As the iced moved, it carried the *Fram* nearer to the North Pole. Nansen almost reached the Pole in 1895, but not quite.

Pole position!

In 1911, the explorer Roald Amundsen and his team were the first people to reach the South Pole.

Who crossed Australia?

The middle of Australia is so hot, it is very hard to travel across. In 1860, Robert Burke and William Wills entered a competition set by the government to cross the middle of Australia. Both explorers starved to death and only one member of their team survived.

Burke and Wills

Who were the first Australians?

Aborigines were the first people to live in Australia. They arrived from Asia over 70,000 years ago. Many Aborigines lived in the Australian outback. Here, it is very hot and dry, and a long way from any big towns.

The *Fram*

Discover

Write a list of all the different animals you would expect to find in Australia.

Did explorers travel by sled?

In 1910, an explorer called Roald Amundsen used dog sleds to travel to the South Pole. Husky dogs pulled the sleds, and if a dog died, it was fed to the other dogs. This reduced the amount of food the men had to carry. Amundsen reached the South Pole in 1911.

Roald Amundsen and his team

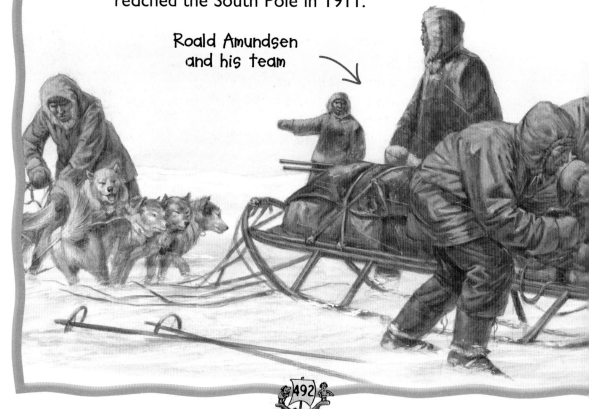

Who conquered Everest?

On 29 May, 1953, Tenzing and Hillary, were the first people to reach the top of Mount Everest, the highest mountain in the world. Since then, many other people have climbed the mountain.

Think

What sports can you play in the ice and snow? Have you tried doing any?

Peary and Henson

How did explorers keep warm at the North Pole?

By wearing sealskins! American explorer Robert Peary and his assistant Matthew Henson wore sealskin clothes when they travelled to the North Pole in 1909. The skins were light, waterproof and very warm. Peary paid local people to make his clothes and equipment.

A mountain of rubbish!

Today Mount Everest is covered in litter and old oxygen tanks left behind by climbers.

Who explored the natural world?

Charles Darwin went on a round-the-world voyage on a ship called the *Beagle*. Darwin was a nature expert and found many new birds, plants, insects and other living things. Once back in England, Darwin wrote important books about the natural world.

Who discovered nine cities?

In 1870, a German called Heinrich Schliemann travelled to Turkey to see if he could find the ancient city of Troy. He discovered the ruins of nine cities, and also dug up piles of beautiful gold jewellery.

Charles Darwin

Going ape!

In 1871, Darwin wrote a book called The Descent of Man. In the book, Darwin said that the very first humans were related to apes.

Which ship explored the seabed?

In 1872, a ship called HMS Challenger set out to explore a new world – the bottom of the sea. The ship measured the seabed, using ropes to find out the depth of the ocean. On its round-the-world voyage, Challenger's crew also found many new kinds of sea creatures.

Draw

You have discovered a new type animal. Draw a picture of it and give it a name.

HMS Challenger

How did people get to the Moon?

In 1969, astronauts travelled to the Moon in a spacecraft called *Apollo 11*. It was launched into space by a huge rocket. It took three days to get to the Moon. Once there, the astronauts spent two hours exploring before flying back to Earth.

Look
Can you see the Moon and stars when you look at the night sky?

Apollo 11

Space animals!

The first astronaut in space wasn't a human, but a dog named Laika. Sadly, Laika died during the voyage, but she led the way for more space exploration.

Who was the first man on the Moon?

The first person to stand on the Moon's surface was American astronaut Neil Armstrong, followed by Buzz Aldrin. They were part of the crew of *Apollo 11*. Both men collected rocks to take back to Earth.

Yuri Gagarin

Who was the first human in space?

In 1961, Yuri Gagarin became the first human to go into space. Gagarin flew around the Earth once in his spacecraft called *Vostok 1*. This took nearly two hours. He then travelled back to Earth and landed safely.

Quiz time

Do you remember what you have read about explorers? These questions will test your memory. The pictures will help you. If you get stuck, read the pages again.

3. Who brought back a giraffe?

page 478

4. Why were spices like gold?

page 479

page 475

1. Who searched for a gold city?

5. Who played a nasty trick?

page 482

page 476

2. Which explorer was very unlucky?

6. How did explorers tell the time?

page 483

page 486

7. Who went on an important mission?

11. Who conquered Everest?
page 493

8. Who was scared by bears?
page 489

12. Who explored the natural world?

page 494

page 497

9. Who tried to get to the North Pole?
page 490

13. Who was the first man on the Moon?

Answers
1. Spanish explorers
2. Ibn Battuta
3. Zheng He Zheng
4. Because they were very valuable
5. The Spanish explorer Francisco Pizarro
6. Using a chronometer
7. Captain James Cook
8. Meriwether Lewis
9. Fridtjof Nansen
10. The Aborigines
11. Tenzing and Hillary
12. Charles Darwin
13. Neil Armstrong

10. Who were the first Australians?
page 491

Index

A

abacus 171, 375
Aborigines 491
Abu Simbel, temple 353
acids 58
aerials 142, 143, 153
Africa 102, 118, 244, 330, 331, 338, 451, 459, 467, 478, 481, 485, 487
agamid lizards 293
air 32, 33, 103, 104, 105, 106, 107, 117, 121, 122, 124, 200, 201, 210
aircraft 137
    Concorde 183
    jumbo jets 168–169
    Red Arrows 169
airships 166–167
alabaster 357
alarm clocks 174
albatrosses 86, 313
Aldrin, Buzz 497
ale 424
algae 72
Algiers 451
alligator snapping turtles 303
alligators 289, 303
alphabet 177, 413
Alps 49, 473
Americas 452, 454, 480–481, 483, 488–489
amphibians 281
    breeding grounds 282, 283
    eaten by reptiles 304
    eggs 284–285
    hibernation 283

Amun Ra, god 352, 353
Amundsen, Roald 491, 492
Anatosaurus 240–241
Andes 49
anemones 73, 79
Angria, Kanhoji 459
animal droppings 254
animals 14, 72, 73, 78, 80–81, 82–83, 84–85, 88, 102, 120, 152–153, 226, 231, 243, 323, 363, 364, 367, 383, 387, 391, 418, 434, 437, 439, 494–495, 497
    fossils 46–47
    grasslands 60
    national parks 65
    rainforests 61
anole lizards 292–293
Antarctica 110, 316, 317
antelopes 345
antlers 417
ants 252
    army ants 267
    food 257
    leafcutter ants 270–271
Anubis, god 352
Apatosaurus 224, 228, 229, 233
apes 345
aphids 257
Apollo 11 spacecraft 496, 497
aqua lungs 94
Arabs 489
arachnids 250
Archaeopteryx 311
archery 424
arches 394
Arctic 43, 310
Arctic hares 336
Arctic Ocean 70, 88
arenas 382–383
Argentinosaurus 227
armour 236, 237, 443
arms 72, 196, 197, 199

Armstrong, Neil 497
army 379, 384–385, 439
arrows 442, 443
arteries 207
Asia 474–475, 479, 481, 485, 491
asteroids 13, 25
astronauts 32–33, 43, 122, 183, 496–497
astronomy 170
Atahuallpa 482
Athens, Greece 125
Atlantic Ocean 70, 113, 481
atmosphere 104–105, 125
atoms 151
Auer, Carl 172
auroras 117
Australia 333, 486, 491
autumn 101
avalanches 111
Avery, Henry 459
axes 442

B

babies 190–191, 204, 238–239, 328, 329, 330, 342, 344, 378
    blue whales 343
    lemmings 336
    opossums 343
baboons 367
Bahamas 480
baileys 434, 437
Baird, John Logie 179
bakeries 435
balance 208
Balboa, Vasco Nuñez de 483
bald eagles 320
baleen plates 80
balloons 123, 169
banded sea snakes 85
Bangladesh 114
banners 445
banquets 372, 373
Barbarossa brothers 450–451
barbers 377, 380
barley 365
barn owls 310–311
barnacles 81
barons 438, 439

bartering 363, 363
Baryonyx 224
basking 280
Bastet, goddess 353
bathing 422–423
baths 380–381, 388, 395
bats 331, 339
batteries 134, 140, 141
battles 442, 443, 444, 445
Battuta, Ibn 476, 477
beadlet anemones 73
beads 421
Beagle 494
beaks 225, 241, 310
beards 450
bears 185, 336, 345, 489
Beaufort Scale 113
bee hummingbirds 313
beer 365
bees 256–257, 344, 364, 391
beetles
  bombardier beetles 265
  click beetles 263
  cockroaches 255
  eggs 254
  fireflies 269
  great diving beetles 269
  tiger beetles 252
Bell, Alexander Graham 177
Benz, Karl 162
Berlin, Emile 178
berserkirs 408
Bible 109
bicycles 163, 192, 193, 214, 215
bills see beaks
birds 86–87, 89, 238, 241, 254, 267, 310–311, 335, 339, 341, 344, 364, 365
  biggest wings 313
  earliest 311
  fastest 314
  largest 312
  smallest 313
  tallest 312
bishops 438
Black Bart (Bartholomew Roberts) 464
black widow spiders 265
blacksmiths 415
blinking 294, 295

blood 197, 206–207
blubber 337
blue whales 80–81, 330–331, 343
board games 381
boats and ships 94, 136, 164–165, 403, 406–407, 427, 473, 477, 480, 483, 485, 488, 490, 494–495
body temperature 280
bone brushes 184
bones 143, 195, 196–197, 198, 209, 214, 241, 244, 314, 323, 417
  food 414
  in houses 412, 423
boneshakers 163
Bonney, Anne 460
boobies 87
Book of Buried Pearls 351
boots 379
bottle banks 65, 155
bottom 198
bowhead whales 334–335
bows and arrows 424
boys 419, 424
Brachiosaurus 226–227
brains 199, 208, 209, 210, 212–213, 227, 233
Brazilian frogs 289
bread 202, 203, 365
breakfast 372
breathing 74, 94, 200–201
breeding 282, 285
breezes 113
Brian Boru, King 426
bricks 394
brides 419
Britain 459, 460
Brush, Charles F. 173
brushes 184
buccaneers 455, 464
bugs 225, 235, 240, 241, 310, 315
buildings 370–371, 380–381, 382–383, 386–387, 388–389, 391, 394
bullet-proof glass 149
Burke, Robert 491
burrows 87
butterflies 252, 275

Apollo butterflies 253
caterpillars 252
colours 254
flying 253
migration 275
monarch butterflies 254–255, 275
painted lady butterflies 275
peacock butterflies 253
wings 253, 254

C

cables 141
cactus 323
caecilians 281, 296
Caillie, René 489
calculators 145
Calicut 479
calves 330, 335, 343
camels 61
cameras 122, 179
candles 175
cane toads 281
canines 204
canoes 488
canyons 17
captains 456, 467
car fumes 64
carbon dioxide 58, 125
Caribbean 43, 453, 455, 458
Caribbean geckos 289
carpenters 366, 467
cars 131, 132, 136, 138, 148, 154, 162
carvings 405
Caspian Sea 55
castles 432–433
  servants 436–437
caterpillars 252, 461
cats 332, 353
cattle 363, 364
cattle horns 424
caves 47, 58–59
cells 193, 197, 207, 213
centipedes 272
Central America 454
central processing units 145
cerebellum 212, 213
cerebrum 212

chainmail 443
Challenger, HMS 495
chameleons 290–291
chariot racing 382, 383
charms 378
Charon 18
cheeks 190
cheese 202
cheetahs 332
chemicals 132, 133
chewing 203
chicken 202
chicks 311, 320, 323
  cuckoos 321
  sandgrouse 322
children 191, 215, 367,
  374–375, 381, 387, 390
chimneys 92
chimpanzees 345
chin 207
China 118, 171, 183, 461, 475,
  477, 478
Christianity 405
chronometers 483
chuckwalla lizards 291
Church 438
churches 405, 441
cicadas 267
cinema 179
Circus Maximus 383
circuses 382–383
cities 136–137, 154
clams 92
Clark, William 488–489
claws 228–229, 231
clay 367
cleaner wrasse 79
cleanliness 371, 380–381, 388,
  395
click beetles 263
clocks 174–175, 483
clothes 149, 376–377, 384, 408,
  415, 420, 439, 463
clouds 23, 62, 106–107, 117,
  122
clownfish 79
clusters 27
Cnut, King 405
coal 155, 466
coal mining 165
coasts 57

coats of arms 444, 445
cochlea 209
cockroaches 255
cocks-of-the-rocks 319
cocoons 258
Coelophysis 235, 241
coffins 359
cold 19, 33, 110, 119, 124, 125,
  192, 193
cold-blooded animals 280–281
collar bones 196
Colombia 467
colonies, termites 259, 261
Colosseum 382–383
colour 17, 23, 27, 116, 117,
  318–319
colouring 75, 83, 87
colours 135, 254, 268, 273
  changing 297
  poisonous frogs 300
  throat pouches 292
  toads 303
Columbus, Christopher
  480–481
combine harvesters 166
combs 417
comets 24–25
compasses 44, 45
Compsognathus 235
computers 140, 144, 173
  electronic brains 145
  Internet 146–147
  railway signals 137
Concorde 183
concrete 137, 197, 382, 392,
  394
conifers 223
continents 70
Cook, Captain James 486–487
cooking 176, 181, 437
  cookers 132, 143
cooks 463, 467
coral 57
  reefs 78–79
coral snakes 297
core 44, 45
corsairs 451, 462
cotton 149, 466
counting 375
counting machines 171
countryside 386–387, 388–389

courtyards 434
Cousteau, Jacques 92
cows 119, 413, 414, 424
crab spiders 271, 273
crabs 72, 85
craftworkers 366
craneflies 270
craters 15, 17, 19, 40, 41
crested water dragons
  302
crests 233
crickets 114
crocodiles 84, 223, 224,
  238, 280
  eggs 286–287, 289
  food 304–305
  hunting 303
  lifespan 305
  'tail-walking' 305
crops 103, 365
crust 44, 45
crystals, snowflakes 52, 53
Cuba (Hispaniola) 453, 455
cubs 329, 340, 342
cuckoos 321
cutlasses 455
Cuzco 482
cycads 223
cyclones 113

D
daddy-long-legs 270
daggers 465
dams 155
dancing 87, 425
Darwin, Charles 494–495
day 11, 15, 42, 43, 100, 101,
  104
deer 329, 333, 344, 24
Deinonychus 228–229
Denmark 402, 405
dermis 193
desert 60–61, 102–103, 109,
  152, 288, 298, 322, 323,
  364
diamonds 467
digging 87
dinner parties 372, 373
Dinosaur Cove 245

dinosaurs 46, 124, 220–221,
    305
  armoured 236–237
  babies 238–239
  biggest 226–227
  cleverest 233
  death 220, 242–243
  eyes 225, 232, 241
  fastest 234–235
  fossils 240, 244–245
  meat-eating 228, 229,
    230–231
  noisiest 233
  plant-eating 222–223, 227
  senses 232
  smallest 235
  teeth 224–225, 230, 231, 244
Diplodocus 227
diseases 243, 263, 485, 486
diving and divers 85, 87, 92,
    94–95
diving beetles 269
doctors 143, 151, 213, 215,
    356, 366, 395
dogs 345, 492, 497
dolls 367
dolphins 224, 334, 341
domes 394
drag boats 94
dragon ships 406–407
dragonflies 262
dragons 289
Drake, Francis 454, 455, 485
dresses 376, 377, 420
drinking horns 424
droppings 240
drought 102, 103
dubbing 441
duck-billed platypus 329
Dunlop, John 163
dust 13, 17, 24, 26, 27, 124
dwarf crocodiles 304

E

eagles 320
ears 197, 208, 209
Earth 12, 13, 17, 19, 20, 24, 31,
    100, 110, 123, 124, 135, 139,
    153, 154–155, 220, 221, 243,
    245

Earth cont.
  atmosphere 104–105, 125
  damaging 64
  day and night 15
  formation of 40–41
  inside 44–45
  inside Earth 14–15
  looking after 65
  probes 34–35
  spinning 42–43
  Sun 10–11
earthquakes 45, 50–51, 390,
    391
earwigs 274
Eastern newts 281
eating 202–203, 214, 215,
    372–373, 385
ebony 466
eclipses 11
ecologists 153
EEG machines 213
eels 79
eggs 77, 87, 89, 238, 239, 243,
    244, 311, 323, 329, 339,
  amphibians 284–285
  bees 257
  butterflies 252
  cuckoos 321
  flies 261
  spiders 258
  reptiles 286–287, 289
  turtles 299
Egypt 108, 472
Egypt, ancient 161, 164, 167
Einar Falsemouth 405
Einstein, Albert 151
El Dorado 475
El Niño 102
electricity 114, 115, 134, 138,
    155, 213
  circuits 141
  mains electricity 140
  refrigerators 180
  wind power 172, 173
elephants 226, 228, 330, 331,
    343, 473
elf owls 323
Elizabeth I 453, 454, 461
emails 146, 147
emeralds 467
emperor penguins 89

enamel 204
enemies 432, 433, 437
energy 132–133, 151
engineers 136
engines 132, 135, 136
engines, jet 168
England 402, 405, 426, 443,
    452–453, 455, 457
epicentre, earthquakes 50
epidermis 193
Erik Bloodaxe, King 404
Erik the Red 403
eruptions, volcanoes 48, 49, 59
Euoplocephalus 237
Europe 479, 485
Everest, Mount 493
exercise 214
exoskeleton 251
experiments 150
extinction 220, 242–243
eyelids 237
eyes 11, 198, 208, 209, 225,
    232, 241, 294, 295, 338, 342
  lens 208
eyes, storms 63
eyesight 317, 323

F

face 199
factories 64
Fahrenheit, Gabriel Daniel
    121
fairy penguins 89
'falx' (knife) 383
family 366
fangs 259
farmers
  animals 413, 414
  longhouses 412
  markets 416
  thunderstorms 411
farming 125, 163, 166–167,
    364–365, 366
farms 388–389
fast food 373
fastest winds 112, 113
fat 202
feasts 425, 427
feathers 233, 241, 310, 314,
    319

feeding 72, 73, 76, 77, 80, 85, 86, 87, 89, 90, 91, 92
feeling 212
feet 72, 86, 87, 196, 316
ferns 221, 223
festivals 427
fighting 73, 81, 231, 382, 384, 385, 417, 419, 424
films 179
fingers 195, 197
fire 51, 161, 176, 433
fire-bellied toads 302–303
fireflies 269
fireworks 132, 183
fish 55, 74–75, 76–77, 79, 87, 92, 202, 203, 224, 240, 317, 335, 415
fish-eating dinosaurs
  Baryonyx 224
  Coelophysis 235, 241
five-lined tree skink lizards 300
flags 464
flats 371
flavours 210, 211
fleas 253, 436
flies 251, 258, 261, 263, 361, 363
flippers 82
floods 108–109, 113, 364
floor mosaics 379
flowers 221, 271, 273, 274, 275, 313
flying 168–169, 310, 314–315
  butterflies 253
  dragonflies 262
  largest bird 313
flying fish 75
flying geckos 291
fogbows 117
follicles 194
food 32, 132–133, 143, 202–203, 204, 205, 210, 211, 214, 372–373, 385, 439, 460, 461, 462, 463
  animals 323
  animal droppings 254
  cooking 176, 181
  crocodiles 304–305
  fish 317, 415
  for animals 414
  honeydew 257

food cont.
  insects 310, 315
  markets 416
  meat 414, 416
  milk 414, 416
  nectar 271, 275, 313
  nuts 310
  refrigerators 180
  snakes 296–297, 301
footprints 244
forces 131, 151
Ford cars 162
forests 61, 64
fortune-telling 391, 393
fossils 46–47, 240, 244–245
foxes 333
Fram 490
France 402, 416, 443
freon gas 180
fresh water 71
friction 131
frilled lizards 293
frogs 281, 304
  breeding grounds 282, 283
  eggs 284–285
  poisons 300–301
  tiniest 289
frost 119
fruit 202, 214, 223, 328, 345, 486, 487
fuel 30
fur 328, 337, 408, 416, 420
furniture 415

G
Gagarin, Yuri 497
galaxies 28–29
Galileo 170
galleys 462–463
Gama, Vasco da 479
games 381
gannets 87, 317
gardens 434
gas 10, 16, 20, 26, 27, 30
  Jupiter 13, 21
  Neptune 13
  Saturn 13, 21
  Uranus 13
gas mantles 172
gases 154, 155

gazelles 332
geckos 289, 290–291, 295
gentoo penguins 89, 316
Germany 416, 421
germs 176, 207, 215, 263
giant clams 92
giant squid 63
giant tortoises 295
Giganotosaurus 231
gills 74
giraffes 226, 363, 363, 478
girls 418
Giza, Egypt 350, 351
glaciers 52–53
gladiators 382, 383
glass 149, 155
  recycling 65
glass beads 421
glasses 171
gloves 192
goats 364
Gobi Desert 475
Goddard, Robert 165
gods and goddesses 352–353, 390–391, 395, 410–411, 425, 427
  Jupiter 390
  Mercury 390, 391
  Mars 390
  Neptune 390, 391
  Venus 390
goggles 95
gold 407, 421, 466, 475, 482, 494
good luck charms 378
government officers 366
graffiti 383
gramophones 178
Grand Gallery, Great Pyramid 351
granite 357
grapes 389
grass 223, 414
grass snakes 301
grasshoppers 267, 273
grasslands 60
gravity 131, 151
Great Barrier Reef 78, 79
great bustards 312
great crested grebes 318
Great Dark Spot 23

Great Pyramid 350–351, 356
great whales 80–81
great white sharks 76
Greece 125, 181
Greenland 402, 403
gripping 190
Groundhog Day 120
groupers 79
groups 226, 240
growing 192, 203
gullet 203
gunpowder 462

H

hailstones 114
hair 193, 194–195, 209, 214,
    328
hairstyles and haircuts 377,
    380, 423
halberds 442
hammerhead sharks 77
hammocks 462
hands 196, 215
Hannibal Barca 473
Harald Bluetooth, King 405
hares 333, 336
harp seals 334
Harrison, John 483
hatching 311
Hatshepsut, Queen 354–355,
    472
Havana 453
Hawaii 487
Hawkins, John 453, 454
hay 414
head 190, 193
headdresses 373, 377
health 214, 215
hearing 209, 213, 232, 285, 294
heart 198, 199, 206–207
heat 10, 16, 19, 26, 27, 33, 103,
    121, 125, 132, 133, 143, 192,
    193
heat sensors 294
heaters 132
heaven 411
helium 123, 167
helmets 409, 444
Henson, Matthew 493
heralds 444–445

herds 226, 240, 343
heroes 425
Herrerasaurus 220–221
hibernation 283
Hillary, Sir Edmund 493
Himalayas 49
hips 197
Hispaniola (Cuba) 453, 455
hives 256
hoes 364
hog-nosed bats 331
holidays 387
honey 256–257, 364
honeydew 257
hornet-moths 267
hornets 266
horns 237
    drinking from 424
horses 234, 383, 410–411, 419,
    439, 440, 441, 442, 445
    combine harvesters 166
    ploughs 167
    railways 163
    rocking horses 185
horsetails 223
hot-air balloons 169
house spiders 266
houses 112, 372–373, 379,
    386–387, 412–413, 415, 423
humans 220
hummingbirds 313, 315
humpback whales 81
Hundred Years War 443
hunters 231, 232, 233
hurricanes 63, 113, 123
hydro power 155
hyenas 338–339, 343

I

ice 13, 52–53, 110, 111, 114,
    117, 125, 490, 492, 493
    comets 24
    Saturn's rings 21
ice skating 53
icebergs 53
Iceland 402
iguanas 85, 295
Iguanodon 229
illnesses 203, 214–215, 373,
    395, 413

Imhotep 356
Incas 482, 484
incisors 204
India 105, 458, 459, 466, 479,
    481
Indian Ocean 70, 113, 458, 459
Indonesia 62
injections 215
ink 374
insect-eating dinosaurs
    Coelophysis 235, 241
    Compsognathus 235
insects 225, 235, 240, 310, 315,
    338, 339, 345
'insulae' (flats) 371
Internet 146–147
intestines 205
Io 20
Ireland 402, 426, 461
iron 44, 138, 466
Isis 109
islands 71
Italy 171, 473, 474
ivory 466

J

jackets 443
Jamaica 457
Janenschia 244–245
Japan 480
jaw 198, 204
Jelling Stone 405
jet engines 168
jets 135
jetskis 95
jewellery 355, 363, 421
    jewellers 366
jewels 378, 459, 467
Jobaria 244
jobs 366–367
joeys 329
joints 197
jumbo jets 168–169
jumping, fleas 253
jungles 152
junks 477
Juno 390
Jupiter 20–21,
    biggest planet 20
    gas 13, 21

Jupiter cont.
  moons 13, 20
  Voyager 1 35

K

kangaroos 329, 333
keeps 435
kelp 83
keratin 195
Khafre, pharaoh 350, 351
Khufu, pharaoh 350
kidneys 207
killer whales 335
kings 404, 425, 426, 436, 437,
  438–439
kitchens 372
kittens 329
knee pads 192
knees 196, 197
knights 436
  fighting 442–443
  heraldry 444–445
  tournaments 441
  training 440–441
knives 383, 465
Komodo dragons 289
krill 80

L

L'Ollonais, Francis 456
laboratories 150
labourers 366
ladies 436, 437
ladybirds 250, 268
Laika 497
lakes 54, 55, 58
lammergeier vultures 323
lamps 160, 172
land 438, 439
lapis lazuli 363
larvae 256
larynx 201
lava 49, 59, 71
Le Clerc, François 453
lead pipes 394
Leaellynasaura 244–245
leafcutter ants 270–271
leaf insects 269
leapfrog 367

learning 191
leather 433
leather jackets 270
leatherback turtles 85, 299
leaves 101, 328, 345, 27
legs 197, 272
lemmings 336
lenses 171
Leoncico 483
leopard seals 83
lessons 374–375
levers 130
Lewis, Meriwether 488–489
life 14
lifespan, crocodiles 305
light 10, 26, 27, 100, 103, 116,
  117, 132, 135, 140, 141,
  142, 208
lighting 160, 172
lightning 114, 115, 141
limestone 149, 357
limpets 72
linen 420, 443
lionfish 79
lions 240, 338, 341, 343
Lippershey, Hans 170
liquid 13, 20, 21
litters 393
Livingstone, Dr 487
lizards, 235, 238, 254, 267, 280,
  315, 323, 339
  dancing 283
  defences 291, 292
  eggs 287
  geckos 289, 290–291
  giant lizards 289
  push-ups 293
  running on two legs 302
  tiniest 289
lobsters 85, 91
locusts 273
longbows 443
longhouses 412, 423
loot 466–467
lords 435, 436–437, 438–439,
  440
lunch 372
lungs 200–201, 206
'Lupercalia' (Valentine's Day)
  387
lyres 375, 381

M

machines 130–131, 137, 140,
  145, 151, 153, 154
Machu Picchu 484
Madagascar 458
Magellan, Ferdinand 485
Maglev trains 165
magma chamber 48
magnets 44, 134, 138–139
  electromagnets 138
  magnetic fields 139, 153
  magnetism 165
Magnus Barelegs 405
Maiasaura 239
maids 436, 437
make-up 376, 421
mammals 328–329
  biggest 330–331
  dangerous 344
  families 340–34, 344
  fastest 332–333
  flying 331
  hunters 344–345,
  sleep 338–339
  smallest 331
  stinkiest 345
  swimmers 334–335
mantle 44
maps 406
marine iguanas 85
markets 363, 416
marriage 419, 423
marrow 197
Mars 16
  moons 13
  probes 35
  red planet 17
materials 137, 148, 149, 150,
  155
maths 171
mating 314, 319
  mating season 292
mayflies 262
meals 372–373, 385
meat 414, 416, 463
meat eaters 304
meat-eating dinosaurs 228,
  229, 230–231
  Deinonychus 228–229
  Giganotosaurus 231

meat-eating dinosaurs cont.
  Rutiodon 223
  Tyrannosaurus rex 224–225,
    230, 231
  Velociraptor 240
medicine 151, 215, 395
Mediterranean 451
Mediterranean Sea 473
meerkats 341
melons 365
men 366
Menkaure, pharaoh 350
Mercury 12
  hot and cold 19
  no moons 13
mermaids 63
messengers 444, 445
metals 44, 148, 155
meteorite 40, 124, 242, 243
mice 339
microchips 145
microscopes 171
microwaves 143, 181
Middle East 416
midges 262
migration 275
milk 328, 329, 343, 414, 416
milksnakes 297
Milky Way 28–29
millipedes 250, 272
mills 435
mining 165
mirages 103
mist 62, 63
moats 433
mobile telephones 142, 147
mock suns 117
molars 204
money 363, 451, 456, 457
monkeys 345
monsoon 105
Moon 11, 13, 18, 40, 41, 43,
  119, 142, 170, 496, 497
  shape changes 15
  wind and rain 19
moonlight 271
moon moths 271
moons 13, 18, 20, 22
moray eels 79
morning star 442
Morocco 476

mosaics 379
mosquitoes 258, 263
mosses 221
moths 258, 263
  moonlight 271
  wings 251
motors 134
mottes 432
Mount Everest 17, 190
mountains 71, 105, 107, 111,
  152, 493
  glaciers 52
  making 49
  ranges 49, 56
  rivers 54, 55
  underwater 56–57
  volcanoes 45, 48
mouth 200, 211
movies 179
mummies 358–359
muscles 198–199, 201, 202,
  203, 205, 206, 208, 213, 214
  birds 314
music 178, 375, 381, 425
Muslims 489
Muttaburrasaurus 235
myriapods 250

N
nails 195
names 405, 408
Nansen, Fridtjof 490
narwhals 81
national parks 65
Native Americans 177,
  488–489
natural world 494
neck 201, 207
nectar 271, 275, 313
Neptune 12
  clouds 23
  gas 13
  Pluto 23
  Voyager 2 34
nerves 199, 208, 213
nests
  ants 270
  birds 311, 320–321
  wasps 259
New World 485

New Zealand 486
newts 281, 284, 292
Nicephore, Joseph 179
night 11, 15, 43, 100, 101, 104
Nile River 108, 364
  crocodiles 287, 305
Njord 411
Noah's ark 109
North America 333, 402
North Pole 101, 336, 490, 493
Northern Lights 117
Norway 402, 404, 405, 490
noses 200, 210, 211, 329, 330
nuclear energy 151
nuts 310

O
O'Malley, Grace 'Baldy' 461
oarfish 75
oases 60
ocean floor 71, 92
  plain 56, 57
ocean sunfish 75
oceans (see seas)
Odin 410
Ohain, Dr Hans von 168
oil 155
old age 214
Old World 485
olives and olive oil 388, 389
Olympus Mons 17
onions 365
opossums 343
orang-utans 328
Ornithomimus 225, 234–235
Ostia 371, 393
ostriches 310, 312–313
ovens, microwave 181
owls 310–311, 323, 391
oxen 364
oxygen 74, 94, 200, 206, 207
oysters 91

P
Pacific Islands 486
Pacific Ocean 70, 102, 113
Packs mammals 231, 240
packs, dinosaurs 345
pain 192

painted lady butterflies 275
'palla' (shawl) 376, 377
pandas 339, 342
pangolins 345
paper 155, 363
   recycling 65
papyrus 363
Parasaurolophus 233
parrot fish 78
pasta 202
Pathfinder 35
peacocks 318–319
pearls 91, 467
Peary, Robert 493
peasants 439
pebbles 223
pelvis 196
penguins 88, 89, 316–317
people 14, 102, 103, 105, 107,
   111, 118, 120
peregrine falcon 314–315
Persian Gulf 467
pets 387
pharaohs 350, 353, 357, 359,
   361, 366
Phoenicians 164, 473
photographs 34, 122, 123,
   179
picture-writing 177
pill millipedes 250
pilot whales 341
pipes 394
pirates 403, 407, 417,
   450–451
   flags 464
   loot 466–467
   ships 462–463
   women pirates 460–461
pistols 465
pivots 130
Pizarro, Francisco 482
plains 71
planes 113, 122–123
   Concorde 183
   jumbo jets 168–169
   Red Arrows 169
planets 12–13, 40, 170
   biggest 20
   dwarf 18
   hottest 16
   red planet 17

plant-eating dinosaurs
   222–223, 227
Apatosaurus 224, 228, 229,
   233
plants 14, 72, 73, 102, 104, 106,
   149, 152, 153, 154, 167, 221,
   224, 237, 243, 271, 273, 274,
   275, 323
   grasslands 60
   national parks 65
   oases 60
   rainforests 61
   water cycle 62
plastic 148, 155
Plateosaurus 222–223
plates 45, 49, 50
playgrounds 130–131
playing 191, 192, 213
ploughs 163, 167, 364
plugs 140
plumage 319
plumb-lines 394
Pluto, dwarf planet 12, 13,
   18, 19
   ice 13
   Charon 18
   Neptune 23
pods 341
poison arrow frogs 300–301
poisons 259, 264, 265
polar bears 88, 336
poles 139, 152
pollen 275
pollution 64, 154
Polo, Marco 474–475
polyps 78
ponds 269, 282, 284, 285
   pondskaters 255
pools, oases 60
Port Royal 457
Portugal 459, 479, 485
power
   hydro power 155
   jet engines 168
   steam power 165
   wind power 172, 173
power stations 140, 154
praying 441
praying mantis 251, 263
prehistoric people 160–161,
   176, 180

priests and priestesses 359, 366
prisms 135
privateers 453
probes 34, 35
pronghorn deer 333
property 366
Protoceratops 237, 238–239
public baths 380–381, 395
puffins 87
Punt 472
pupas 252
pupils 208, 209
pups 77, 337
pylons 141
pyramids 350, 356–357
Pytheas 483
pythons 297

Q
quarrels 417
queens 257, 261, 436, 438–439

R
Ra, Sun god 352
rabbits 329
Rackham, 'Calico Jack' 460
radar 137
radio 123, 142, 143
radio waves 137, 142–143, 153
raids 407
railways 163, 165
   signals 137
rain 19, 58, 60, 62–63, 102,
   103, 104, 105, 106–107,
   110, 121
   floods 113, 108–109
   rain dances 118, 119
rainbows 116–117, 135
rainforest 61, 104, 328, 24, 310,
   319
ramps 130
Ramses II, pharaoh 353
ranges, mountains 49, 56
raptors 233
rat tail fish 92
ratsnakes 296–297
rattlesnakes 294
rays 72
Read, Mary 460

recycling 64, 65
Red Arrows 169
red kangaroos 333
red pandas 339
Red Sea 92, 459
reefs 78–79
  coral 57
reflexes 190
refrigerators 180
reptiles 84–85
  eggs 286–287, 289
  living underground 296
retrievers 442
rhinoceroses 344-345
ribs 196, 201
riches 357, 366
Richter Scale, earthquakes
  51
rings
  Neptune 23
  Saturn 21
  Uranus 23
Riojasaurus 223
rivers 54–55, 106, 108, 109,
  152, 285
roadrunners 315
roads 384, 392
'Robbers' (board game) 381
Roberts, Bartholomew 'Black
  Bart' 464
robes 444
robots 34–35
rock 15, 19, 25
  Earth 13, 14–15
  Mars 13, 17, 35
  Mercury 13
  shooting stars 24
  Venus 13
rockets 30, 31, 496
Rockies 49
rocking horses 185
rocks 139, 242, 243, 244, 245
  caves 58–59
  coasts 57
  crumbling 47
  fossils 46–47
  making the Earth 40
  volcanoes 48, 49
  waterfalls 54
Roman Empire 370, 384, 392
Romans 168

Rome 370–371, 382–383, 393,
  394, 395, 473
Roosevelt, Theodore 185
roots 195, 204
Royal Navy 460
royal pythons 297
rubber 148, 149
rubies 467
Rudel, Jaufre 441
runes 413
running 198, 201, 213, 310, 315
Russia 402, 416, 417
Rutiodon 223

S

sagas 425
Sahara Desert 102
sailors 473, 477, 481, 483, 485,
  486
sails 164–165
salamanders 281
salmon 55
salt 91
saltwater crocodiles 84
San Francisco 51
sand 149
sand lizards 283
sand tiger sharks 77
sandals 373, 379
sandgrouse 322
Santa 427
Santa Maria 480
sapphires 467
sarcophagus 359
satellites 123, 142
Saturn 12, 35
  gas 13, 21
  moons 13
  rings 21
sauropods 226, 227, 229
scales 345
scavengers 231
Schliemann, Heinrich 494
school 374–375, 390, 418
schools of fish 74
schooners 462
science 130, 136, 137
scientists 46, 56, 131, 136,
  150, 151–152, 153, 154,
  155, 245

Scooter 23
scorpions 264–265
Scotland 402, 426, 483
scuba divers 94
scurvy 485, 486
sea 102, 106, 245, 405, 415,
  417
  sea water 71, 73, 84, 90, 91
  seabed 495
sea anemones 73, 79
sea creatures 243
sea dogs 454
sea lions 82
sea monsters 63
sea otters 83
sea snakes 85
sea spiders 92, 63
sea turtles 299
seabirds 86–87, 89
seahorses 78
seals 76, 82, 83, 334, 335,
  337
sealskin clothes 493
seamounts 71
seas and oceans 41, 152
  coasts 57
  icebergs 53
  mountains under 56–57
  rain 62–63
  rivers 54
  temperatures 43
seasnakes 299
seaweed 83, 85, 90
seeds 27
see-saws 130–131
senses 212, 213
sensors 192, 193, 208, 209,
  210, 211
servants 436, 437
sharks 76–77
shaving 354
shawls 376, 377
shears 377
sheep 364, 414
shellfish 29, 72, 81, 85, 91, 92,
  415
shells
  eggs 286
  tortoises 295
  turtles 299
Shetland Islands 427

shields 408, 409, 419, 444
Shih, Ching 461
shins 196
ships 403, 406–407, 427,
    462–463
ships and sailing 391, 393
shirts 420
shoes 379, 443
shooting stars 24
shopping centres 371
shops 147
shoulder blades 196
shrews 243
shrines 391
shuttles 30–31
sidewinding vipers 298
sight 208, 232
silk 459, 466
silk, spiders 258, 275
silver 454, 457, 466
singing 201, 319
Skadi 411
skateboards 192, 193
skeleton 196–197
skin 192–193, 194, 209, 214,
    280, 281
  colours 292
  frills 293
  poisonous frogs 300
  shedding 301
skink lizards 300
skull 196
skull-and-crossbones 464
skunks 344, 345
skyscrapers 136, 137
slaves 388, 393, 407, 451
sleds 492
sleep 33, 83, 86, 283, 462
sloth bears 345
smell 210, 211, 213, 329, 232,
    333
smiling 199
smoke signals 177
snakes 315, 323, 280
  changing colour 297
  eggs 287
  jaws 301
  killing prey 296–297
  living underground 296
  seasnakes 299
  shedding skin 301

snakes cont.
  sidewinding vipers 298
  swallowing food 301
  tongues 294
snow 110–111, 118
snowflakes 52, 53, 110, 111
sockets 140
soda 149
soil 35, 245, 364, 365
Sojourner 35
Solar System 12, 16, 20, 25, 35
soldier termites 261
soldiers 360–361, 379, 384–385,
    433, 439, 442, 443, 444, 445
Somalia 354
song thrushes 311
songs 81, 83, 63
sound 132, 135, 201, 209
South America 49, 61, 482,
    484
South China Seas 459
South Pole 101, 491, 492
space 124, 143, 151, 170, 242,
    243
space rockets 43
space shuttle 182
space stations 183
space travel 16, 19, 21
  astronauts 32–33
  robots 34–35
  shuttles 30–31
  spacecraft 10, 16, 21, 32–33,
    122, 496–497
  spacesuits 19, 33
spadefoot toads 281
Spain 452–453, 454, 475,
    482–483, 485
spawn 284
speaking 211, 213
spears 424
spectacles 171
speed 135, 142
Spencer, Percy L. 181
sphinx 351
spices 459, 466, 479, 485
spiders 250, 252, 267
  black widow spiders 265
  crab spiders 271, 273
  fangs 259
  garden spiders 250
  house spiders 266

spiders cont.
  poisons 265
  silk 258, 275
  spitting spiders 258
  tarantulas 265
  webs 258–259, 275
spindles 134
spinning tops 367
sponges 73
sports 380, 424
spring 100
squid 86, 63, 335
squires 440, 441
Sri Lanka 466
stalactites and stalagmites 59
Stanley, Henry 487
starfish 72, 85
stars 10, 24, 170
  galaxies 28–29
  how stars are made 26–27
steam baths 422–423
steam power 165
steel 137, 138, 197
Stephenson, George 165
stewards 437
stick insects 269
stings 257, 264
'stola' (dress) 376, 377
stomach 203, 205
stone 357, 433
Stone Age people 160, 180
stone tools 160
  carved 405
stories 425
storms 62, 63, 112, 113, 390,
    391
  Jupiter 20
  Mars 17
  Neptune 23
streams 58
street lights 172
streets 393
Styracosaurus 237
submarines 56, 143
Sumerians 161, 177
summer 100, 101
sums 145
Sun 10–11, 12, 13, 15, 19, 23,
    24, 40, 43, 47, 100, 101, 104,
    109, 117, 124, 125, 135, 155,
    481, 486

Sun cont.
  asteroid belt 25
  star 26, 27
  sunspots 11
sun dogs 117
sunbathing 280
sundials 175
surfing 95
Surinam toads 285
Svein Forkbeard 405
swallowing 203, 205
sweat 193
Sweden 100, 402
swifts 314, 315
swimming 75, 76, 82, 84, 85,
  88, 89, 310, 316, 317
swimming, snakes 299
switches 141
Switzerland 442
swords 408, 409, 419, 424, 440,
  441, 442

T

'Tables' (board game) 381
tadpoles 284
Tahiti 486
tails 227, 237
'tail-walking', crocodiles 305
takeaways 373
Tanzania 487
tarantulas 265
tarsiers 338
taste 210, 211, 213, 232
  taste buds 211
teachers 440
teddy bears 185
teeth 198, 204, 224–225, 230,
  231, 244, 310
telephones 177
telescopes 170
television 140, 142, 143, 179
temperatures 110, 121, 122,
  133
temples 353, 391, 395
tentacles 79, 63
Tenzing, Sherpa 493
termites 259, 261, 345
'testudo' (tortoise) 385
thermometers 121, 133
thighs 196

thinking 212, 213
Thor 411
Thorfinn Skullsplitter 405
thorn bugs 273
'Three Stones' (board game)
  381
thresher sharks 77
throat pouches 292
thunderstorms 62, 112,
  114–115, 141, 411
Tiber river 393
tiger beetles 252
tiger sharks 77
tigers 344
tiles 379
Timbuktu 489
time 151, 174–175
  telling the time 483
toads 281, 283, 284, 285, 303
toes 195, 197
togas 376
toilets 181, 371, 395, 413
tombs 350, 355
  tomb robbers 351, 355
tongues 211, 290–291, 294,
  303
tools 60, 415
toothbrushes 184
tornadoes 63, 112
tortoises 280, 288, 295, 385
tortoiseshell 118
touch 192, 193, 213, 232
tournaments 441
Tower of Winds 125
towers 435
towns 111, 417
toys 185, 367, 415
tractors 163
trade 363–363, 366
trains 131, 136, 137, 163, 165
Trajan's Market 371
transport 392–393
treasure 402, 403, 407, 417,
  451, 455, 458, 459, 462, 465,
  467
trees 101, 112, 125, 149, 221,
  223, 389
  rainforests 61
trenches 71
Triceratops 236, 237
trilobites 46–47

Tripoli, Countess of 441
Troodon 232–233
tropical countries 62
tropics 104
trousers 384, 420
Troy 494
trunks 331
tuataras 280
tube worms 92, 63
tunics 384, 420, 443
turbines 173
Turkey 47, 494
turtles 84, 85, 280, 299,
  303
tusks 81
Twyford, Thomas 181
typhoons 113
Tyrannosaurus rex 224–225, 230,
  231
tyres 163

U

underground living 296
underwater village 92
United States of America 103,
  120, 485, 488–489
Uranus 12, 22–23
  gas 13
  moons 22
  Voyager 2 34
urine 207

V

Valentine's Day 387
vegetables 202, 214
veins 207
Velociraptor 240
Venus 12, 17, 486
  hottest planet 16
  no moons 13
Vikings 34, 481
villages 415, 437
villas 372–373, 379, 386–387
vines 389
Vinland 481
vipers 298
Virginia opossums 343
viziers 366, 367
voice 201

volcanoes 14, 71, 45, 242, 243
 biggest 17
 Io 20
 eruptions 48, 49, 59
 lava caves 59
 underwater 56, 57
Vostok I spacecraft 497
Voyager I 35
Voyager 2 34
vultures 322–323

W

Wales 426, 443
walking 191, 198
walls 433, 434, 435
walruses 82, 83
wandering albatrosses 86
warriors 402, 407, 408, 411
washing 33, 215, 436
washing machines 140
wasps 259
waste 155, 205, 207
 recycling 64, 65
watches 175
water 10, 14, 32, 33, 41, 107,
 110, 114, 117, 122, 133, 143,
 155, 322, 323, 364–365, 435,
 462, 463
 caves 58–59
 in deserts 60–61
 lakes 55
 rain 58, 60, 62–63
 rivers 54–55
 water pipes 394, 395
water cycle 106
water dragons 302
water, walking on 255
waterfalls 54
waterskiing 94
waves 57
weapons 385, 409, 415, 419,
 424, 465

weather 104, 118, 154, 221,
 243
 changing 125
 dinosaurs 124
 drought 102, 103
 floods 113, 108–109
 forecasting 122–123
 monsoon 105
 rain 102, 103, 104, 105,
 106–107, 110, 121
 rainbows 116–117
 rainforests 61
 sayings 119
 snow 110–111, 118
 storms 62, 53
 thunderstorms 112, 114–115
 wind 112–113, 118, 120, 122,
 125
weather houses 121
weather vanes 120–121, 125
weaver birds 321
web pages 146
webs 258–259, 275
Weddell seals 335
weight 32, 131
west 120
West Indies 481
whales 80–81, 330–331,
 334–335, 341, 483
wheat 365
wheels 131, 161, 163, 174
Whittle, Sir Frank 168
wigs 377
wild dogs 345
Wills, William 491
wind 19, 63, 112–113, 118, 120,
 122, 125, 155
windmills 172, 173
windows 149
windpipe 200, 201
wine 365
wings 251, 310, 314, 315
 albatrosses 313

wings cont.
 butterflies 253, 254
 crickets 260
 penguins 316
wingspans 86
winter 100, 101
wires 134, 138
wolves 333, 340–341
women 366
 at war 409
 clothes 420
 hairstyles 423
 marriage 419, 423
 older women 419
wood 149, 363, 367, 433
woodlice 252
wool 415, 416, 420, 443
words 177, 427
workers 257, 261, 356–357
World Wide Web 146, 147
worms 252
worship 390–391, 395
wrist watches 175
writing 177

X

X-rays 143
Xuan-Zang 477

Y

yellow-bellied sea snakes 85
Yule 427

Z

Zheng He Zheng 478
zips 184